Waiting for the
MARTIAN
EXPRESS

Waiting for the
MARTIAN EXPRESS

Cosmic Visitors, Earth Warriors, Luminous Dreams

RICHARD GROSSINGER

North Atlantic Books
Berkeley, California

Waiting for the Martian Express:
Cosmic Visitors, Earth Warriors, Luminous Dreams

Copyright © 1989 by Richard Grossinger

ISBN 1-55643-052-3 (cloth)
ISBN 1-55643-051-5 (paperback)

Published by North Atlantic Books
          2800 Woolsey Street
          Berkeley, California 94705

Cover art by Ruth Terrill
Cover and book design by Paula Morrison
Typeset by Classic Typography

Waiting for the Martian Express: Cosmic Visitors, Earth Warriors,
Luminous Dreams is sponsored by the Society for the Study of Native
Arts and Sciences, a nonprofit educational corporation whose goals are
to develop an ecological and crosscultural perspective linking various
scientific, social, and artistic fields; to nurture a holistic view of arts,
sciences, humanities, and healing; and to publish and distribute literature
on the relationship of mind, body, and nature.

Library of Congress Cataloging-in-Publication Data

Grossinger, Richard, 1944–
    Waiting for the Martian express: cosmic visitors, earth warriors,
luminous dreams / Richard Grossinger.
        p.   cm.
    Bibliography: p.
    Includes index.
    ISBN 1-55643-052-3 : $20.00. — ISBN 1-55643-051-5 (pbk.) : $9.95
    1. New Age movement—Controversial literature.   2. United States—
Civilization—1970-   3. United States—Social conditions—1980-
I. Title.
BP605.N48G77   1989
133—dc19   89-3009
                                                                      CIP

For my aunts and great-aunts, Suzanne Taylor, Anne Metzger,
Dorothy Nassberg, Ruth Zises, in acknowledgement of their care

Acknowledgements

"Waiting for the Martian Express" and "Third World Wipeout" were originally essays in *The Unfinished Business of Doctor Hermes* (published in 1976). These expanded and edited versions include sections from other essays in the same book as well as from author's earlier collection *Martian Homecoming at the All-American Revival Church* (1974).

"Deep Numerical Music" first appeared in *The Slag of Creation* (1975).

"The Brazilian Master in Berkeley" first appeared in *Co-Evolution Quarterly* (Number 38, Summer, 1983) under the title "Capoeira: A Martial Art from the Streets and Jungles of Brazil Comes North."

"The Return of the Warrior," "Aboriginal Elder Speaks in Ojai," and "Easy Death" all appeared in *Planetary Mysteries*, edited by Richard Grossinger (1986). "Easy Death" also appeared in *East-West Journal* (Volume 14, Number 11, November, 1984), and a small section of "Aboriginal Elder in Ojai" appeared in *East-West Journal* (Volume 15, Number 1, January, 1985) in a version prepared and rewritten by them and not authorized by the author. (The editor of *East-West Journal* could not accept the critical tone of the piece but still wanted to publish an account of the conference.)

"About the Bomb" first appeared as the Preface to *Nuclear Strategy and the Code of the Warrior: Faces of Mars and Shiva in the Crisis of Human Survival*, edited by Richard Grossinger and Lindy Hough (1984).

The "Letter to the MacArthur Foundation" was finally mailed in January, 1988. A one-sentence reply thanked the writer for his letter which was "read with interest."

"The Face on Mars" first appeared as the Publisher's Foreword to *The Monuments on Mars: A City on the Edge of Forever* by Richard C. Hoagland (1987).

"Giving Them a Name" was delivered as a paper at the "Angels, Aliens, and Archetypes" Conference, sponsored by Omega Foundation, Palace of Fine Arts, San Francisco, November, 1987.

The first version of "A Critical Look at the New Age" was taped as a talk at Arthur Young's Institute for the Study of Consciousness, Berkeley, December, 1987.

"The Mind of the Heart" first appeared in the Foreword to the 1987 edition of *Planet Medicine: From Stone-Age Shamanism to Post-Industrial Healing.*

"Luminous Dreams" first appeared as a section of "The Dream Work" in *Dreams Are Wiser Than Men*, edited by Richard Russo (1987).

With the exception of "Giving Them a Name," "The Mind of the Heart," and "Luminous Dreams," all of the materials that appeared elsewhere were edited and rewritten for this book. Very minor revisions were also made in the above.

Contents

SEA WALL

We all have histories. There is a way that we got here, a path through time to the moment when the text begins.

For some their history seems to go back to past lives. It is not clear whether they experience these lives as a nuance or an actuality.

And how would we know? The ways we have of telling ourselves who we are do not contain any information about truly how long we have existed. ("Bridey Murphy" was only an exercise—one way of tracing back through the records of the brain. An informal briefing. Such exercises teach us that memory itself is murky, that even the simplest episodes rearrange themselves in layers and distort hopelessly.)

Some scientists claim that dreams are no more than the biocomputer of the brain erasing itself—ridding the mind of unneeded static. So, the whole realm of nighttime symbolism is eradicated by decree. But if dreams are no more than erasure, what is life itself? Is it not the ceaseless activity of erasure, parting the waves to create this present moment of fiction? The biocomputer erasing only to re-record? Is any living thing saved?

When the flesh itself is finally destroyed, does anything but vacancy flow into the field of the stars?

This present existence begins in the twinkling of babyhood, the signs of which are lost in the babble of languagelessness. Childhood is a memory. It is also a memory of a memory, and memory of a memory of a memory. From this moment, at which the waves part, there are many versions of childhood, memories of memories, echoing without break back into the mist of personal beginnings. Where there is no memory, there is still the intuition of continuity, or what psychologists call "unconscious memory." The appearance of continuity does not just retreat to a beginning at which it is excised. It combines and overrides; in seeming to go backward it actually goes everywhere, sealing our entry point into this narrative. We may have only brief and fragmentary memories of the earliest days of childhood, but our sense of our own eternal being-ness is as strong there as it is in memories of yesterday. We seem to ourselves very much as the universe seems to us: originless—sealed by walls of gravity, light, and time-space, or sealed by shadows, warp, and the fiction of personal history.

We are born into a circumstance of beings, and define our-selves in reference to others like us. But this is supposition. Our existences could be any number of other things too. This life is shrouded in mystery, certainly all other existences imaginarily lived by the same being too. How many of the memories of childhood are true memories, real déjà vû, as opposed to the language of memory in which we recreate ourselves for adult purposes?

For a world of so much light, for such a bright concrete world, this place is a hoax. Only its appearance is bright, only the sur-face, the textured subsurfaces. Otherwise, we live among shad-ows . . . all of our existence, among shadows, the majority of peo-ple submerged, acting out what they imagine or tell themselves is real. Nothing is so obvious as that almost no one (and none of this) is awake. We project our lives against a vast screen which, although no longer explicitly astrological and feudal, is just as infinitesimalizing.

We cannot get inside of time. But we cannot go out of time either.

Other than a biological stream of being, recognized in the laws of thermodynamics and the beating of our heart-lung ma-chine, time does not exist.

Without metabolism, our movement through "time" would

be like our movement through space, except one-way. We would wander from place to place in time, forever. Death would be all-the-same, only elsewhere.

What do we struggle for when we embrace and adore our lives (as against dying)? Is it the illusion of continuity?; the preservation of meaning?; a forgotten promise?; the revenge of undying love?

Each moment is already eternal. Each moment lives forever; all others are obliterated and absorbed. In breathing we pass from one immortality to another, as phenomena.

When we die, memory is reclaimed by time. Memory was just cells; language the grope of nerve tissue toward discourse.

Between us and eternity lies an ocean of unconscious melody that cannot be crossed, so (over aeons—and episodes) must only be born. The immortal moment lies outside of time, evolving beyond words.

As we get older our life spreads out into actual timelessness. The dot of present location erodes; prior decades deteriorate and lose their discrete days, wrapping around the single moments of youth like waterbugs around insects' bodies on the surface of a pond. Aging perplexes the romance of a simple plot, an adventurous climb through time and space; our sustenance always came more from single clarities than the stream of existence anyway.

We are lost in time-space even as we would be, cut adrift in spacesuits between planets, left to float for as long as our food, drink, and air sustain us. Yet the universe appears to have a beginning and an end as it surrounds us. Termini upon a mirage.

*   *   *

An East German playwright surmised that there are no real tragedies in the West. "The only tragedy of the twentieth century," he said privately, " is the failure of Marxism. All other stories are melodrama."

This means, for instance, that a narrative called "The Making of a Sandinista" has the possibility of being real because a student gives up his bourgeois identity and goes into the northern mountains of Nicaragua to join the small band of guerrillas gathering against Somoza. After his training, he declares himself a new man; the mountains and the mud and the rain have worn away his prior individual existence; he is now a collective being, feeling happiness and sorrow in the context of his people (the communal being) rather than his own selfish personhood.

With all the misery and injustice in the world—and with the present exploitation of the poor and weak—it hardly seems possible to be a hero without regard to the destiny of the masses. What is one life, unlinked to collective humanity? Why tell a story of love or romance or even transcendence in the West if all it leads to is another consumer, another generation of consumers? Another story to be consumed? Another "Dallas" (which is only the epitome of a self-aggrandizement universalized)?

What heroisms are there not corrupted by vanity and hunger for goods? What desire evokes eros without addiction? Where can a love affair occur except against a backdrop of starving billions, slaughtered animals, and poisoned jungles?

As much as one would like to report a cleansing nihilism in the West, we are more evidently confronted by a reborn greed for goods, a new religion of "looking out for number one," made all the more trenchant by its flimsiness in the present crisis. Even the exiled Tibetan guru brings to the West only a stern warning regarding "spiritual materialism," that mind-set in which one acquires blessings, holy attributes, mantras, future lives, even as one acquires foreign cars and fine artwork. One acquires romance likewise.

These enhanced individual lives consume and are consumed, their bodies deprogrammed by the hospitals and disposed of by the funeral constabulary. At least in the Mediaeval milieu the society followed the fate of the king as the pieces on a chessboard do. When the Habsburg prince Maximilian set out from Vienna to Ghent in 1477 to claim his bride the Princess Marie, and with her the Holy Roman Emperorship, he was a poor man with barely an entourage. But as he travelled, he was met by cheering mobs in the towns and villages along the way and presented with gifts of great value. During his three-month journey the wedding procession swelled, and by the time he and his retinue marched through the circle of wind-mills surrounding the city, up to the palace, he was arrayed in borrowed armor and wore a garland of pearls and precious stones on his blond hair. The banners in the streets read: "Most glorious prince, defend us or we perish." He did, for more than 400 years, and look what arose from the tatters of his dynasty. . . .

We have since evolved. Modern society is not only future society; it is a society without subplots. Mao, the Shah, Marcos. . . . Cosmos follows cosmos like TV serials, as we are ground in the machinery of our own institutions. The Moon is no longer the Moon. We have now achieved a nuclear denouement to represent the dull balance by which we are all anyway held.

The German playwright did not necessarily sanction the story of the Sandinista, nor did he glorify the state of operas of the Eastern Bloc and Red Guards. These too are petty heroisms. They end up serving corrupt military bureaucracies, which are as materialist and decadent as the Western marketplace and transnational corporations. He said specifically that the tragedy was the "*failure of Marxism.*" That is, we have become communal only in ways that continue to exploit the majority of creatures of the Earth. We have become communal consumers, global exporters; we have hardly advanced beyond the economics of the slave trade. The governments of nations are no more than big cosa nostras—the Russian Revolution having deteriorated into a crime syndicate armed with tanks and nuclear warheads, and Ronald Reagan more explicable as a mob boss protecting his territory and ill-gotten loot than as a descendant of Jefferson guarding democratic institutions.

Is it no wonder that we are all literally "communists" even as we are all potential consumers? The poorest of all refugees have become independent businessmen in Central California or won (or lost) some other twentieth-century lottery.

When word of starvation in Africa reached the West through the Commonwealth media, a campaign was initiated to transport some of the temporary abundance of North America to its sister continent. It turned out to be extremely difficult to enact something even as logistically unidimensional as gathering food in one port, shipping it to another, and distributing it inland from there. A large quantity of goods was apparently interdicted by the military regime of Ethiopia, fighting an old tribal war against Eritrea, within the boundaries of Italian Northern Africa.

The money for the food was raised in part by a chorus of rock stars singing: "We are the World." Bruce Springsteen, Bob Dylan, Tina Turner, Madonna. . . . The intended message was communalist in the best sense: we—all of us—are—each of us—the world.

But when the Moon is no longer the Moon, such literal equations are mere propaganda. No astronomer-goldsmith will spend ten years fashioning an orrery of gold for the child prince. Our kings are dead of overdoses, and there are too many of us, the mythologies that lead us too fragmentary ever to recombine.

We now recognize the single being of humanity—all of us cloned like holograms from the same print of amino acids, going back to ancient Egypt, China, and beyond, to stone and ice ages. We bear replica melodies within these many bodies. When Dylan, Madonna, and beautiful blind Stevie Wonder sang, "We are the World," they meant just that. The song haunts us not because *we* are the world but because they are, because *they* provide an illusion of princes and princesses whose liaisons and collective fame might rescue us from a crisis larger than our lives.

Likewise, when a movie actress discovers her former existences as kings and queens and priestesses, we also seem to live forever; we imagine it is possible to be reincarnated, to be famous, to be royalty. WE ARE THE WORLD. And this means *everyone*—not just actresses—all the people of the world once priestesses, highwaymen, and knights.

Is it not strange? Is it not most of all strange that it might all be or not be—all of it, none of it—those dying in Africa, those never growing up in Africa, those not even being born, anywhere—living again, or not living again, as kings or queens, as rock stars or insects, or simply the deliquescent fabric of a hydrogen-carbon universe?

1986

THE NEW AGE

1. The Sixties, Seventies, and Eighties

There is no "New Age," or every age is a "New Age." Every randomly defined period of history is (of course) "new" when it is happening; yet all periods of history are subject to the eternal return of events and meanings. If we try to name the features by which observers declare a present New Age, we find only some of the oldest and most conservative human activities: millennialism, the sacred Earth, channelling and mediumship, communication with nonhuman entities, ritual participation in food and medicine, faith healing, and shamanism. These were also hallmarks of the so-called sixties revival, a New Age which was partially eclipsed by the materialism of the late seventies.

It is clear that the present New Age includes those aspects of sixties culture that deepened and spread, plus some significant changes in value and orientation. For instance, hallucinogens were popular during the sixties, but seekers in the eighties prefer mediums for their otherworldly trips. Drugs have been exposed as addictive and superficial (though not as universally and categorically as the current teetotallers would like to convince us). Activists in the sixties and early seventies specialized in anti-war rallies and street theater; those in the eighties have on the one hand joined the political establishment and on the other launched clandestine Earth First! and Animal Liberation guerrillas. Meanwhile, computers and telecommunications have broken down barriers and spread information (even top secret) throughout the planet; the control of the State has eroded, and the so-called superpowers have been forced to collaborate to preserve a few more decades of their hegemony.

The psychelic imagery of the sixties has been diluted, but in its place is a more widespread and serious inroad into mainstream culture. While certain features of Aquarian culture have matured into viable institutions, others have spawned full-scale plagues. The recyclable energy systems and small farms that decorated the ideal sixties landscape have been tested and integrated into the economy and even made the policy of a global party (Greens). The array of windmills at Altamont Pass resembles an Aquarian army displaced more (still) from the future than from the past. The hardcore communes have, for the most part, dispersed; their role is partially filled by sectarian camps and retreats. People do not as easily write the radical proclamation with their lives, preferring seminars to fulltime living commitments, personal identity to group identity, guided growth to spontaneous breakthrough. But the communal "cults" of Rajneesh, Hare Krishna, and Reverend Moon are utter reversals of the freewheeling utopian farms of the sixties. From Rainbow Gatherings and Deadheads to urban panhandlers and crack gangs, the decay of the Western logos is now severe and inevitable. These are not oldtime rock groupies and social workers. They are truly the Vandals and the Huns.

The sixties pretty much accepted institutional medicine while initiating alternative schools and farms. The eighties have exposed the medical and scientific establishments and begun holistic self-care programs. Buddhists have come to the West and set up strict trainings which many have willingly undergone, yielding some of their attachment to easy revelation and enlightenment. The sixties' sequinned goddesses and Indian robes have progressed into hologrammatic paradoxes and taos of physics. The original New Age was mythological and pancultural; the later one has a theosophical and science-fiction ring.

Woodstock deteriorated into punk and then reestablished itself as "We Are The World," Farm Aid, and Harmonic Convergence. While the Aquarians spoke of peace and centering, the present era now seeks the actual grounding of Feldenkrais somatics, t'ai chi ch'uan, and aikido. Overaggressive peace-mongering has been exposed as part of the cycle of war; conversely, those who fought in Vietnam are viewed now more as the victims than the provocateurs. The inquiry into "Peace and Conflict" has been formalized, and comparatively more effort is going into comprehending the nature of the violence in us than into attacking the Pentagon. And the internal discipline and service of warriorship has been established as something different from the military. The Warrior Network, First Earth Battalion, and Guardian Angels have outflanked even the draft and the "pigs." Note Lomi School founder Richard Heckler training the Green Berets in aikido and meditation, and finding them more zen, more "peace"-oriented than the local Marxist professors.

But there is also a new vanity and superficiality, a loss of sensuality and consciousness. Joggers with electronic gauges and miniaturized tape decks have supplanted poets, jugglers, and street artists. Manicured and tailored babies in fashion carriages have replaced longhaired funky kids in overalls and hand-me-downs. The sixties were blatant in how their partisans rebelled against the killer culture and stormed heaven's gate; the eighties have rebounded in shock and denial, and many of their partisans (in some cases the same people) now shun the sparc and revolutionary lifestyle to punch in at the mirage of the economic revival and bottomless Asian market.

The effort to acquire and have "a good time" has been revived as something much more robotized and synthetic than during the cotillion and beach-party fifties. Nothing will bring back Beaver and the Nelsons, and the pretence to Ward Cleaver merely leads to Ivan Boesky, the pretence to Audie Murphy gives us Ollie North. No more "back to the future." Because we have used up everything . . . because we are tired of waiting . . . because we want to test the absolute bottom line before it vanishes into cosmic debt. Insider trading, cocaine dealing, airport terrorism, and ever higher-priced superstars are all different faces of the same desperate grasp at the ungauged infinity, while there is still matter left to grasp. Superman is now the Terminator, Donald Duck the self-conscious Roger Rabbit. When we try to elect Dwight Eisenhower, we get Ronald Reagan (the movie). Every attempt to be more poignant and real seems to make us less human, as though there are only mannikins and cartoon figures left in our repertoire. No wonder Stanley Kubrick ended *Full Metal Jacket* with the Marines marching out of Hué singing the "Mickey Mouse Club" song. At the same time we reach back nostalgically to the last glimmers of innocent joy that united us, we acknowledge that we are following an animated caricature of humanity across the jungles of Asia.

2. Science and Pseudoscience

The original New Age drew its material and inspiration from such ancient and longstanding systems as alchemy, Buddhism, Taoism, astrology, and the works of technologically simple people. Because these practices had never been synthesized in the context of one another and a global society, their rediscovery and application in the sixties made for a "New Age." In general, as the industrial culture of universal scientism disintegrates, original spiritual practices reappear in novel forms. Unable to integrate the activities of the "potential movement" without losing its own identity, institutional science blames them on a combination of wishful thinking and poor education, at the same time dismissing them as superstitious and hiring hit-men to blow them away. But New Age practitioners define themselves by this ghettoization: "We may not be scientists and skeptics," they say, "but we are in touch with our humanity and with the greater rhythms of the cosmos that override epochal science." There is arrogance and provinciality mixed with the wisdom in that stance.

In fact, many New Age beliefs *are* uneducated, unexamined pseudoscience: imitations and metaphors of scientific language are tossed off as if unassailable fact. For instance (and typically enough), the editor of José Argüelles' "Harmonic Convergence" wrote me recently (responding to some of the essays in this book): "Like Argüelles (sic), the cosmos and my own cells are luminous, filled with spiraling energy. I do not comprehend what it is to feel alone. You are a circular thinker, I am a spiraling thinker. It is almost as if we have completely different DNA." ("Who goes around giving out the spiral-thinker academy awards?" I responded. "I think all our cells are luminous and filled with spiraling energy, not just yours and José's.") Because science is based on hermeticism and archetypal thinking (Pythagoras and Democritus, and ultimately, even Kepler and Newton), it is always subject to primary occult derivations. When these occult uses of science are not just stale slogans (or personal inflations, as above), they can be visionary and empowering. And that should not be a problem, except to doctrinal purists.

Meanwhile, a righteous and self-proclaimed objectivity has filtered from mass science into mass culture as a form of artificial life-making that infects the New Age equally. The lives that people in the West have come to accept during the nineteenth and twentieth centuries are often reflections of machines and bureaucracies, academic and political rigidities. People unconsciously perceive themselves as statistics, as products, as consumers, as molecular repositories of knowledge and professions, as enactors of styles and values. This general hypnosis is celebrated in beer and perfume ads, by couples on holiday, and in the melodramas people borrow—as if their own—from movies and magazines. One acquires enjoyment rather than enjoys; note the presumption of "quality time," as if life flowed in even punch clock packets. We have made ourselves equations of experimental hedonism, marathon runners chasing behind or after midlife crises.

Yet, existence is a thing that is spontaneous and beyond definition. When we ignore its hidden aspect our lives become automatic, and we seek fulfillment only externally and superficially. A careful reading of the Buddhist and Western esoteric traditions which helped spawn the Aquarian revival would deliver the same warning. The professions and public and civic goals of the twentieth century may yet be reflections of an inner transit, but one that has become utterly obscure.

3. New Age Marketing

To my understanding, "New Age" in the best sense involves an intention to experience and explore the interior of creation, beyond secular biological existence. The New Age has also committed itself to feed the starving people in Africa and Asia; to preserve our soil and atmosphere (and elephants, tigers, and whales) for future generations; to rescue the rain forests; and to end the arms race— commitments which suggest that we are better than we have thus far shown, that we are still capable of walking off the edge of history. We know that it is impossible; yet we also know it must occur, that things cannot go on forever like this. We may support such an agenda for humanist, religious, or spiritual reasons, but it amounts to the same intention toward radical change. Those people who seek it may be at total odds with one another, but then their conflicts are also part of the intention toward change.

In the light of all this, what is the New Age at which this book takes a critical look? Why is it that so much constructive and well-meaning activity requires criticism?

The answer is: the actual New Age is not at stake here; the world must change according to esoteric principles at its core. But the marketed New Age is at best a series of well-meaning simplifica- tions and at worst a hustle and a fraud made possible by those simplifications. It is the marketing of the New Age, the invention of attractive mirages, the promulgation of clichés, that this book addresses. A *true* cultural and spiritual revival is our only hope.

One New Age hallmark is an unexamined belief in sacred geometry and geography. Crystals and pyramids are presumed to harbor and transmit power, though their mechanism is unknown. Pil- grims flock to old Indian ruins and Southern temple sites as if these were the storage centers of palpable chi energy. The recent proc- lamation of a "harmonic convergence" in the Solar System was a grandiose version of the same numerology and archetypalism.

I don't see any reason to reject entirely the potential of crystals and pyramids or to debunk the flow of undiscovered energies through lei lines and between power points. In fact, these areas of inquiry hold much promise for the future. I suspect that big technologies in the universe are not run by fossil-fuel machines or nuclear power, or even by computers and superconductors, but arise from elemental mind/matter. Homoeopathy's success in treat- ing patients with an "impossible" system of spiritualized pharmacy is an indication of the potential of vitalistic mechanics (though neither "vitalistic" nor "mechanics" may describe what is at stake). However, there is a difference between passively hanging crystals around one's neck to receive healing and internalizing the traditional lore of such stones in native cultures on a shamanic and experiential basis. There is also a difference between engaging with subtle rhythms and changes on a daily basis of study and meditation and gathering on a single day to proclaim a harmonic dividing line in history.

The uninvolved commitment to a New Age becomes simply an escape to hypothetical enlightenment without having to participate in the mess and dissolution of the world. Activities like praying before the rising sun and gathering in groups to celebrate the mystery of the cosmos should be practices, not one-shot holidays. The words "love" and "peace" in and of themselves are phonetic lisps and mean nothing. They can represent heartfelt desires, but they can also, as Freud and Reich showed, reflect irritations, neuroses, and character armor that work against the very goals they denote. Harmonic convergences are counterproductive to the degree that they distract people from the real issues. They are like Fourth of July celebrations and rock concerts—on the calendar mainly to promote ideology and commerce.

As recent political escapees from Eastern Europe and the Soviet Union have noted, the West is debilitating in that it presents endless trivial choices—what toothpaste, what breakfast cereal, what shirt? People lose their lives in distinctions that have no meaning and no potential. "America" is just one version of a modern tyranny of ideology and bureaucracy—sometimes in the name of choice, sometimes in the name of the socialist revolution, but always in the name of conformity and the abstract power of economics. The danger is that sacred crystals have become like toothpastes, rock concerts like patriotic parades.

4. Millennialism

In our imaginary (cumulative) New Age holy book, life (and the universe) are a Gothic tale with plots and subplots (including angels, extraterrestrials, Atlanteans, intelligent sea mammals, Yetis,

Indian guides, spirits taking turns taking over bodies and speaking oracularly, magical temples, messages left in pyramids, multidimensional travel, past-life evolution, the Second Coming, and the like). The New Age is not yet a commitment to the unknown nature of reality or our own novel experience; it is a screenplay for events that have supposedly been programmed and foreshadowed, narrated to us by those who have already lived. This kind of on-high prophecy seems pretentious and elitist in the face of our actual condition.

The atmosphere and oceans continue to be contaminated and degraded; exotic—almost pornographic—weaponry multiplies on a global scale. This world is not even perceived as real by entrepreneurs and state terrorists; what can we then expect from transcendentals? (If the world is not ultimate reality, the New Age implicitly argues, then how could the stage on which it is played be important? The tired seas and skies will crack like cheap porcelain and be replaced by many new dimensions of space-time. The Rosicrucians thought likewise in 1618, at the onset of a Thirty Years War).

There are now drug skirmishes on the streets of North America. Tens of thousands of people wander homeless. And the terrorism of the rest is all too blatant. In the midst of our New Age renaissance lurks a greedy, know-nothing, caring-little-for-life culture that murders recreationally and racially and is wed to the basest of goods and displays. If you don't like a referee's call in neighborhood hoops, butcher him. If someone cuts in front of you on the highway—son of a bitch, gun him down.

Yet this is vintage New Age: death followed always by rebirth, life by more life, degradation before evolution, Pisces unto Aries. How conveniently the dead Elvis and John Lennon are reconstituted and sighted on the mean streets! The New Age method of dealing with "big" problems too closely resembles the Armageddon copout, so tellingly cited by James Watt when he was queried about the consequences of using up our natural resources. The innocent victims of urban crime and terrorist explosives merely choose new bodies and return to the fray.

It is almost as though the very arguments used to affirm that

the universe is benign and souls are eternal have become rational-
izations for a brute and gaudy materialism, for trashing this ter-
rain and wasting its bodies. The "Ivan Boesky's," crack salesmen,
and so-called yuppies still insist on their right to life style at the
expense of anyone and everyone; the Fundamentalist scientists and
Christians still fight each other to impose their separate versions
of idolatry on the patriotic masses—though all these activities must
end in emptiness against this century's hollow background.

(The motivation behind New Age millennialism is suspiciously
self-serving. Even if some of the apocalyptic scenarios intend to
accelerate our evolution and rescue the whole planet, others have
the same mean-spirited impetus as right-wing religious propaganda
and chain letters: the faithful can barely wait for catastrophe
because they expect to be its beneficiaries. So they send out letters from the Florida Keys claiming to be channels for Abraham
Maslow, delightedly confirming the dates of Nostradamus' earthquakes, in the guise of warnings. But what is passed off as un-
sullied prophecy merely masks unconscious curse.)

In addition, the various rescues by aliens, earthquakes, and
economic collapses that have partial New Age allegiance (depend-
ing upon one's affiliations) are denials of the complexity and commitment of life. It is not that they couldn't happen; it is that they
are not real. The biological process that underlies this world is
profound and serious and represents a covenant with the divine
force; it cannot be abrogated from other dimensions. If there is
a macrocosm and a microcosm, these are not separated by great
walls or even master geometries; they are joined a billion times
more intimately than the minute branching and impregnation of
nerves and flesh. If mere images and words are shattered between
cosmoses, certainly our apologies redeem nothing. The Buddhist
response of compassion and sorrow is still more appropriate than
the New Age one of awaiting mutation and rescue.

5. Channels

There is also a "New Age" tendency to accept fairly standard conceits about cosmic and personal evolution from a variety of mediumistic channels. It is unclear whether the sources of these "spirit"

messages are truly external and if external whether they are located on this planet, but additionally there is the problem of their content which is either overly pat and clichéd or utterly obscure— leading one to question why any evolved being would go through the trouble to initiate such communications. Given the obvious difference between any embodied and disembodied worlds, real transmissions from spirits and the dead should be succinct and pithy. Yet you can find material identical to most of this channelling of multithousand-year-old beings in any second-rate metaphysics or theosophy book from the last five hundred years.

If you don't believe that a yuppie Madison Avenue has taken over the image-making of heaven, consider that one of the wholesalers of Da Free John's work recently suggested to the publisher (Dawn Horse Press) that the books would sell far better if the information were presented as channelled rather than from a living master. We hardly need the debunkers given the job the New Age is doing on itself.

If someone is dead, is he or she necessarily wiser? Is not our present condition so extraordinary that the words of a living master are quite miraculous enough? The implication that the glimpse beyond death is so enlightening it alone transcends any earthly enlightenment tends to trivialize both this life and the fact of dying, linking them in a trivial spy network. The whole thing smacks of Iron Curtains and ham radios.

Channelled messages are often trite and impractical (heavy on "peace" and "love" and "evolution" which cannot be experienced except abstractly or enacted except as preached instructions), compared, for instance, to poetry which arises from muses that are not explicitly disembodied. By taking into account the opacity and intrinsic paradox of language, poetry is often much more mysterious and true to the riddle of our existence. The process of submitting one's path to automatic writing or a spirit is not necessarily trivial, but the continuous popularizing of such messages and the overall channelling phenomenon suggest a dangerously literal interpretation of the universe.

For instance, through mediums the spirits tell us such things as: Mankind is evolving but needs to break the cycle of violence and express the love implicit in all. They tell us our identity does not rest in mind or body but in spirit. They tell us that America is the forerunner of a new Jerusalem (or Lemuria). They tell us that we are God's very design, and if we act from natural good instinct we will develop the better qualities of the universe. They tell us to summon healing from our heart and send it through our arteries and neurons. They tell us reality is self-created—even bad reality. We can end our self-pity and create new reality any time (they do not mean to sound condescending, but this can even be done by blacks in South Africa and starving children in Cambodia and Bangladesh). They tell us to create new energy patterns, that 99% of our being is already in communication with the other dimensions. They tell us there is a difference between female energy and woman. They tell us that male and female are primary poles in the cosmos, and should engage creatively. They tell us brain-mind, sufficient energy, its own field, manifests in some reality, allow the goddess to co-create. They tell us there are beings on other worlds and in other dimensions, watching and aiding us, that they themselves are. They tell us that the landscapes of stars and planets are extensions of God's love. They tell us that if we needed to feel guilty in this life we chose parents and a situation that would make us so. They tell us the Atlanteans could fly and change bodies, that they held the key to anti-gravity-and transmutation. They promise they will meet us in the mountains of Peru. They say it is all radiant light, and we are light. They tell us that through many lifetimes, certainly. . . . They tell us dragonfly, sylph, subtle energy, angel, stone circle, aura, sacred shield, Osiris, cell hologram, with shining hair.

There is nothing malign or even unenlightened about these communications; they are in fact good gospel, but at the same time static, impersonal, and sanctimonious. They don't grapple. They suggest that the path has been provided. If this wisdom could be followed literally and unambiguously, channelling would be a tool transcending any church or science. But insurmountable difficulties arise when one tries to take the content of these messages into lives. They cannot serve as a rallying-point for any real change or growth. Compare these conceits to selected lines of contempoary poets:

"Who bury the dead/lead forth the bride/stainless in dress." (Gerrit Lansing).

"Hail and beware the dead who will talk life until you are blue/in the face. And you will not understand what is wrong. . . ." (Charles Olson).

"There is no life that does not rise/melodic from the scales of the marvelous./To which our grief refers." (Robert Duncan).

"I dip my hand in yours and eat your flesh/you are my mirror image and my sister/you disappear like smoke on misty hills." (Diane di Prima).

"you're a long way gone from here, Billy/body becoming earth and the rest of you farther than star light/messages across the green glaciers of interstellar drift." (Lenore Kandel).

"To them we are weird while to us/They are not weird, to them we are undeniable." (Edward Dorn).

"Nothing but/comes and goes/in a moment." (Robert Creeley).

"There is something in me which is not open, it does not wish to live/it is dying/But then in the sun, looking out to sea/center upon center unfold/lotus petals, the/boundless waves of bliss." (Joanne Kyger).

"whose name is love & which only of all light love can eat." (Robert Kelly).

If the cosmos is presented as a finished thesis in a mediumistic context, then authority takes precedent over experience. And there is no place to go with such law, no way to generate new form and experience. Only when there is a feeling of unfathomable mystery and a sense of wonder do we change and affect the world. By language alone poetry represents active perception and life. Channelling represents frozen dogma and piety. Yet poetry books are virtually unsellable and channelled works have become our present godspeech and epitaph.

6. Crazy Wisdom

In truth, there is no simple plot to follow or set of instructions which will break down the paradoxes and contradictions of existence. The world is strange, and we are confronted, from the depths of the genetic code through the unconscious mind, with intuitions and transmissions of unknown relevance that inspire our growth and change. All human scripts begin in the middle of nowhere and end without resolution; this is as true for the formulas of physics as it is for the proclamations of Seth or Lazaris. The problem is not the channelled information itself but the illusion that its content explains our circumstance. The gods have chosen to be tricksters first, authorities never. Many Buddhist masters, Da Free John and Chögyam Trungpa included, have been assailed for their so-called crazy wisdom. Trungpa had disciples carry him around naked at a party; broke antennas off cars on a city street and handed them to a student; spent days speaking in spoonerisms. Assuming that the ego, the programmed mind will subvert any material it is given—even the most shocking prophecies and pronouncements—these masters attempt to wake people through extreme behavior which challenges the basis of daily reality. While the New Age guru imposes a narrative on our lives and offers change through dramatic, cosmic events, the "crazy wisdom" teacher interrupts the mindflow of self-image and social role; even a visit from the Martians would be less radical and disruptive.

This is a culture which already puts its faith in Biblical prescriptions that are removed from experience and do not require inner transformation or real understanding. Sacred verses are worshipped by their arbitrary numbers, the numerals paraded like totems at public events. They are insignias of combat and division, not mantras. The actual prescriptions of Christ demand radical change (giving up of wealth, following of a spiritual path), but people pay lip service to them, as to channelled messages, and seem not to care, therefore, whether preachers engage in hoarding of goods, corruption, and kinky sex with prostitutes. Jimmy Swaggart's lapses, by reinforcing conventional notions of addiction and sexual neurosis, are actually the opposite of "crazy wisdom." Note that Swaggart simplifies Jesus in much the way mediums simplify spirits. He acts out blatant perversions in direct contradiction to his own preachings and then announces he has been forgiven. Does not our whole species act with equal hypocrisy with regard to war, genocide, and the despoliation of our planet? It is no wonder that New Age clichés and Christian Fundamentalism war for the allegiance of the same decade.

7. The Attack on the New Age

The reaction against simple reincarnative thinking should not lead automatically to nihilism or existential sparseness. Yes, there is a usefulness to Samuel Beckett's vision of the deterioration of memory and loss of human capacity in that it is a creative realization of an aspect of nature that makes "New Ageism" ludicrous and trivial by comparison, but to live and die in that minimal way does not really lead to internalization and growth (though to write about it does):

"If there's one question I dread, to which I've never been able to invent a satisfactory reply, it's the question, 'What am I doing?'"[1]

Part of our existence must be to invent our lives and deaths, and New Age thinking can be a step in that direction when it is individual and its vision is authentic. It is usually far preferable to those systems which attack it—progressive scientism and conservative religiosity. The former, in its least appealing and so-called humanistic guise (as professional skeptics and debunkers), is set up not so much to condemn blatant frauds as to discourage people from any form of inquiry other than approved scientism; it is purely and simply a religion, an orthodox religion with claims of salvation (albeit secular) but only if the Commandment is followed absolutely. Of course, science is self-defined as universal objective inquiry; thus, it assumes that any true study will come under its scrutiny and be subjected to its tests. In an ideal instance science is as experiential as Buddhism, but in actuality science is a closely guarded set of professional covens in which only already sanctioned truths are permitted. Professional skeptics are actually proud of their unwillingness to engage in paranormal experimentations (instead, they attend only to debunk).

On the other side, the Christian fundamentalists attack the New Age as pantheistic, a heresy equal, from their perspective, to scientism. The Christian attack (like the scientific one) is totalitarian—to prevent people from having experiences that might lead them to other systems of belief. Even various New Age groups are intolerant of each other and of "down time," when the organism just drifts from day to day, unknowing. We comprise a civilization in which competing bureaucratic religions and political systems seek our total adherence and try to interest us in pledging our existences, our lives (and eternities) to their credos and roles.

8. Reincarnation and the Soul

People are truly bewildered; they go from accepting death as the end to believing that they have lived many times before. They take on the stories of other existences like movie scripts; therefore, this life must read to them like a movie script too. What is missing, in this guise of mythological immortality, is a sense of the bottomless sorrow of existence (including rebirth if need be), a sense of the pure carnal desire drawing one into life and through it, a sense of fear and agony before a nature which simply consumes. It is no fun to be on this roller coaster, but it is also bewitching, exhilirating, and charged with an intimation of the bigness of how the universe might be. In that sense, the sheer experience of the paradox of one life can be as powerful an insight into the reality of the universe as a recovery of innumerable other lives—so it almost doesn't matter if this is the only life or one in a series. The fear of death—the fear of annihilation of the ego—may be our actual experience of immortality in that it is more intrinsic than any artificial and wishful projection of immortality; it is close to the heart of our existence.

There are also truths that arise from traditional meditation and other forms of inquiry that have to do with the fact of being *in* the universe. Because these come from the core of who and what we are, they have a truth that no science-fiction story can. If the other lives are not there and we face a hollowness, then great beauty and even immortality are born of that hollowness. Sorrow has real texture; dismay roots us at the heart. In bodywork, often lethargy and lack of focus, a kind of dreariness, lead to the soul quicker than exhilarating hits of pounding and release. We float in our own static and substance, between hunger and satiety, between (Faulkner) grief and nothing. This is the true bottomlessness of existence which is coeval to the bottomlessness of indivisible matter or the endlessness of the galaxies of stars.

Our culture has become in general so externalized and so dependent on events that we tend to invent outward manifestations of things which only happen internally and over great periods of time. We are in a hurry to complete evolution, to make contact with extraterrestrials, to live, die, get reborn, relive previous lives, and be done with it (although to what end and what next we are uncertain). We evade the basic somatic fact of living and the commitment to the sullen and wild blue creation from which the real wonders of the cosmos come unplanned, unnamed, and often unnoticed. The sheer fact of life, the experience of love beyond sacristy contains within it a coincidence and a vibration so powerful that cultural hype tends to be a distraction. The irony is that as we strive toward the cosmic we lose the cosmic, we replace the experience of profundity with the artificial projection of profundity onto shallow events.

1988

WAITING FOR
THE MARTIAN EXPRESS

from *Martian Homecoming at the All-American Revival Church* and *The Unfinished Buisness of Doctor Hermes*

In the 1950s the Indian Rope Trick met Western science: "They collected several hundred people and a Fakir to put on the show. All of the observers, including the scientists, saw the Fakir throw a coil of rope in the air and saw a small boy climb up the rope and disappear. Subsequently dismembered parts of this small boy came tumbling down to the ground, the Fakir gathered them up in the basket, ascended the rope, and both the boy and the Fakir came down smiling. It is astonishing that several hundred people witnessed this demonstration and agreed in general on the details as described. There was not a single person present in the crowd who could deny these facts. However, when the motion pictures of this scene were developed subsequently, it was found that the Fakir had walked into the center of the group of people and thrown the rope in the air, but that it had fallen to the ground. The Fakir and his boy assistant had stood motionless by the rope through the rest of the demonstration. The rope did not stay in the air, the body did not ascend the rope."[1] Andrija Puharich.

— Collective hallucination — proclaimed the scientists, the same smug enthusiasm with which they greeted long-lost coelecanth and out-of-orbit Pluto, with which they later invited the Brazilian shaman to lecture at Palo Alto and the Hindu philosopher to demonstrate the position of black holes in the Vedas. — We are learning

23

more and more—they told themselves as their telescopes chased the speed of light to the ends of time-space illusion, to the birth of nature itself in a quark of dust. But then things got really difficult.

"He took by the shoulder a man standing next to him and without a word plunged a paring knife (a very sharp four-inch stainless steel blade with a cocobolo wood handle) toward the man's left eyeball.

"The knife was skillfully inserted under the upper eyelid, and the sharp point plunged deep into the eye socket. The patient was calm and relaxed, and when queried as to possible pain, he answered that he felt nothing. Arigó then pressed the point of the knife up through the upper chamber of the eye socket so that the point lifted the skin above the eye (supraorbital forehead area). Arigó asked me to feel the point of the knife through the skin, which I did. I affirmed that I could palpate the sharp tip of the knife. This exercise lasted about twenty seconds. When the knife was withdrawn from the eye socket, I asked the patient how he felt. He replied that he felt normal. Examination of the eye did not reveal any laceration, redness or other signs of irritation. . . .

"The patients stood in a long line waiting to see Arigó. When one stepped up, Arigó looked up at him or her from his desk, asked no questions, and in a few seconds began a definitive treatment, either surgical or medical, on each of the two hundred patients. He sent a dozen patients away, saying that their problems could easily be handled by any medical doctor. He performed eye surgery and ear surgery on ten patients, each operation averaging about thirty seconds. He used the same knife on each patient and wiped it on his shirt after each operation. . . . . . . bleeding was minimal; and each patient walked out of the room by himself after surgery."[2]

Jule Eisenbud was there too. He saw it all. He returned to Colorado, to his psychoanalytic practice; without ceremony he put aside the text on telepathy, which was to have been his last. If anything Arigó had confirmed what he suspected all along.

"What could I say that would mean anything? These things happen. They're real. We're someplace else. We're on the outside looking in."

He is not unhappy. He is calm and resigned. "Why should I have the final word?" he asks. "What does a cat think? Do we know what's in the mind of that tree as it grows?" The tree, whose leaves reach up from the garden into night. "How did the stars look to the Babylonians? What in god's name did they think those things were up there?"

His cat climbs the fence and jumps into the tree, sits beside the Moon, chesire. The catalpa blossoms blow gently against the twilight, light as snow; they spin in the water of a fountain he once built.

"How did we get here, Richard? If this is the world, what are we doing here? Is it fear? Or is it something else I can't *quite* put my finger on?"

He would like to write music, perhaps some poetry. He would like to put away, for Western man, the need to prove, to come up with comprehensive theories, to explain what will be there in any case, at the end as at the beginning. For he can look back over his life and see that he was never a Babylonian; all his work was for society, in society's terms, was to keep him from being in touch with powers in himself he studied the parallel of in others.

"The only conclusion," Jule says, "is that all which is possible is possible with the mind as well."

*　　*　　*

We have measured the shape of the galaxy from within, separating by radio waves the arms from the center. We have detected the faint incoming whisper of a supergalaxy, with a galactic center, around which the Milky Way, Andromeda, the Magellanic Clouds, move in orbit. As we approach the star-suns, whose billions of atomic explosions per cubic inch per light second are the breath of life, we lose the differential that makes us real. In our tables of law the universe began with such an explosion. All our body-minds were elemental hydrogen, and have arrived here by a cooling, a slowing down, a jelling, a condensation. The pre-Socratics, closer to that explosion than we, caught its spirit in their writings: "Neither in speculation nor in actuality can we ever know the number of things that are separated out" (Anaxagoras).

We have imagined neutron stars, white dwarfs, black holes, rough patches of original stellar gas, particles on the other side of the speed of light. They do not relieve our boredom; they do not locate us any better; they pass from fiction through mathematics into physics, and there they hang, unproven and unrelieved. "In everything there is a portion of everything else, except of mind," writes Anaxagoras; "and in some things there is mind also."[3]

We have imagined the birth of this planet in a nebula, its death in a nebula. To neither were we witness. We have sent ourselves on million-year space voyages and returned from hibernation and dilation unchanged.

We have seen Newton's firm matter, and with it our flesh and bones, deteriorate into particles which are mere vibrations, are substanceless, proving that even as Newton is Democritus relived, Pythagoras returns as Heisenberg, citing the call letters of an invisible harp. Where solidity vanishes, it is replaced by the guards of the castle, guards so flimsy, so Platonic, and stationed so far apart, it is clear we shall never enter the castle at all.

The abstractions of science have become so powerful they engulf any possible objects. Though our civilization has changed tremendously in its use of the planet's energy, our relationship to sky and mind is unchanged. It is the illusion we live in an enlightened age, we have a cosmic perspective, that prevents us, as much as anything, from perceiving our occasion. Descendants of pyramid-builders and numerologists, we are still trapped in triangles and circles.

The darkness of the sky, the stars in it spread thin, the prophecy in Hubble's Law of an expanding universe. The national debt, the population. The age of *Homo Africanus.* The nuclear stockpiles. Two thousand tanks, manufactured in the U.S. and U.S.S.R., enacting a reptilian battle in the Sinai.

"But you are the author of this story," says the daydream to the dreamer. "There is no suspense. *You* can dash us into the sun, or find a black hole between the orbits of Venus and Mercury; you can steer us through to the Earthlike planet where we begin again. Why pretend to be a mere passenger, or a victim?"

"You know," Jule says, "the psychoanalytic interpretation of star-fascination?"

"Stars to offset loss," he answers himself. "Because they return; because they are permanent. Great panic when great change in the sky."

But where do they come from? Surely we did not imagine ourselves in such a universe? Surely they are real, are not the distant reflected dross of our neurons? "Do not be too sure," says Einstein, backhandedly echoing Aleister Crowley, echoing the *Pymander*, echoing lost Hermes.

"An infinity without," Jule says, "to protect us against the infinity within."

*   *   *

People have been waiting for the change, but while they have been waiting they have been changing. In darkness Saturn passes through gates for which we have no name. Old father Saturn who, without being Chronos, is time.

And we were thinking once to go so far, in Rosicrucian terms, in science-fiction measurements of time and space, in the Asia retrograde shadow over the West, that now we are seen, as the shadow of the obelisk in a remote star, not to have moved at all.

Those things we despised we are becoming. Fires lit of loose childhood trash and mimeo proclamations and kundalini promises and fifties rock-and-roll visions, have burned all they are going to burn; they are burning out.

The Martians have come and gone. Their presence, at one time as simple as the space ships they commandeered, the appointments they kept, is now one more relic of history. Might as well put them in a museum with Bali masks and sections of Mayan stellae — as obscure and as final to our being here as the Hittites and Beothuks, yet as familiar as Flash Gordon, the late great Flash Gordon, conquistador and Cosmic Intelligence Agency dupe.

For all their presence, their distance is the more complete echo and when we hear it in *Chariot of the Gods*, we recall that one misplaced messenger hides another always in a sequence of broken contacts. Or is it still the misplaced concreteness Whitehead assigns to us as incorrigible materialists, the so-called broken contact between local DNA and its possible sires out in the cosmos? Surely they weren't a gang of blond, bearded warriors in anti-gravity ships playing a big brass band. But does that make them Minoans, Phoenicians, Norsemen? One mystery, one lost tribe, is as obligatory as another: Easter Island "magicians," Semite sailors, Celtic tree-priests, the peoples who farmed Southeast Asia in post-glacial summer, ancestral to us and without whom *we* could not exist.

For all our crash programs we cannot bring the Martians into world politics and theology; we cannot bid them to teach us their solar and wind technologies, their mind machines, or how to get unhooked from global oil economics. They will have nothing to do with the way in which we built the atomic bomb or made it to the Moon. They are in no such hurry; they decline all our Super-bowl offers — even when we promise this will be the last one, win-ner take all. "We are different," they say, without having to say it. They know us for the compulsive gamblers we are.

But equally, we cannot dismiss them. For all their broken promises, their stubborn silences when we needed proof, they re-main. And though their echo is so faint it might not exist at all, we hear it. If it is not theirs, it is still an echo. And when we point to the revelations of the future, the power sciences and medicines yet to come, we have the sobering intuition these are the bare minutiae of the arts and religions of the past.

We have been misled by the hermetic as by the scientific; what is easy has been made forever hard. And in its place we have the difficult solved, but to what end? And we keep asking: is it an alternative form of energy, a massage so light the fingers are not even touching, a solution so dilute it is nonchemical? Is that how subtle must be our penance for the grossest of sins? And will it work? Will it give increased energy?

Our nightmare of overpopulation, of dwindling resources, is our vision of the life-box we have put ourselves into. The stars unfold a lesson daily we seem not to regard, either in scale or in-tensity, because day to day we work only to get to the end of it, to give our lives back to the butcher because the streets are filled with them, homeless, unemployed. We have the medicine of that type of system. Fire-extinguisher medicine. We have a life limited metabolically to our expectations. Anything else would be too much, would lead to madness, and then they'd come in with the big mindbending drugs.

In the ruins of sexual freedom and anarchy, guilt ascends, its signs on every porn theatre and playland, no matter how hard they try to blast it out: FUN, LIBERATION. They gird their leather boots and drag in the corpses for the necrophiliacs. Our obsession with light brings us, procedurally, to darkness. The decadence may be incredibly complicated, even sensuous. But it has no remedies in it; it doesn't even have a pure skeleton of a human body or a magnetic needle. They are not happy. It is the mummy's curse.

Few people see that this was the only real message of the Manson cult. I agree, they fucked it up entirely, and continue to. But they said: delight in darkness, for darkness is coming; they said: darkness be gentle to us and we will be your agents. Ecstatic participation in the downfall of Western consciousness. They were not into ritual murder or sex orgies; they were not interested in the devil per se. They embraced, ostensibly for all of us, the disorder that surrounds us and is implicit in each day's careen. If they failed, it was because they underestimated how big Western consciousness was, how it owned them too, and used their actions as petty pornography and crime. It said: —You've got a long way to go before you get out of me—. And they agreed.

Although I can't find a place where any one of them put it in so many words, it seems to me that underneath all of African pre-Socratic philosophy is the addendum: Men are not immortal because they will not let themselves be. Not that men are not deep enough. Not that men are not able to feel deep enough. Heraclitus: "Most people do not take heed of the things they encounter, nor do they grasp them even when they have learned about them, although they think they do."[4] . . . . they think they do. . . .

*   *   *

We live in a world that has passed, though its flourishes ring out like the banners of passing armies. It owns TV networks, stadiums, newspapers, publishing companies, computers, refineries; it smells of expensive shaving lotion and dresses in five-hundred-dollar suits. Its transportation systems and office buildings carry it through these dangerous times unharmed. Everywhere it looks, it sees itself: a muscle man, a general with wings and stars, or a handsome diplomat of attractive ethnic charm, a record-setting Olympic athlete, boyish in his enthusiasm. How is he to know? The city lights gleam tonight as on all nights: the machinery processes an ever-new chemistry of fabrics and medicines. Vital, dynamic, smiling like Charlemagne. Surrounded on all sides by ancient undefeated peoples. The certainty of neon all around us, sign after road sign gleaming in the night; lights roaring by, on the radio *Cathy's Clown.*

*   *   *

Now Puharich is at the balcony of the Tel Aviv Hilton; his guide and associate: Uri Geller. Horus pursues and guards them. Seven flares drop through the sky, seven plumes of white smoke.

— You may use the name Spectra for us, but we are not Spectra. That is the name of an artificial world we have placed invisibly above the Earth for eight hundred years. We are from another galaxy; we are gods and create worlds without end — .

Who is speaking with whose voice? How do they know everything we think as we think it, everything we were before we became it? Why do they sound exactly like our invention of them, and then disappear? How do they travel the uncrossable distances between islands of stars?

— Your race is anxious and unacceptable. Your mind is too small for the immensity of the cosmos — .

Uri bending spoons, stopping the clocks in the school playground because they have been with him all his life. . . . because they were also the hands behind Arigó's hands, and now they answer with the dead Brazilian's voice: — No, the automobile accident did not hurt me — .

Now Andrija and Uri are in the Israeli desert, awaiting a wine-red spaceship to appear among the stars. Spotting it, Puharich breathes a sigh of relief. Visitation on schedule.

— Andrija, stop — pleads Uri. — Listen to me. I'm your contact with them — . "I know you and you know me. . . . But nobody really knows anybody. We don't know this Spectra at all, Andrija. . . . . look at the foolish things they are doing. Sometimes they say 'You definitely must go!' and then they change their minds! Andrija, you understand? To us it looks like they are not stable, goddammit. They are so powerful, yet they are not stable. And maybe that unstableness that we think of them . . . maybe for them it is nothing. Maybe for them it's just a breath, you know. For them it's nothing, but we feel it — like suddenly for two to four months we don't receive anything from them because we're not together. Maybe for them it was just turning around — to see something, and back at us again. Maybe for them it was just stopping a computer for a second, a split second, and for us it was a month. Now we don't know their timing, their difference from us, their character. We don't know anything about them. So we're not allowed to! You know, Andrija. . . . sometimes I get the feeling — what if all this is just a big joke? Andrija, what if they are clowns? What if this whole thing that is happening to us — it's just one little clown that has run away from the king's garden, and he's playing with us because he has those powers? What if it's that? What if it's not at all a big, huge, godlike thing. . . . What if Hoova is just a goddamn little clown that is playing with us?"[5]

This is more than a Martian Homecoming; it is like the original story Frederick Brown gave us forty years ago. *Martians, Go Home.* Diminutive Casper-the-Ghost creatures who spied on everyone and gave away everyone's secrets. Turning world conflict into world collaboration. Now, at the precise moment of holocaust, manipulating Anwar Sadat's brain. Not to *prevent* the Arab-Israeli War, but to let it fall on the correct cosmic-astrological date.

*   *   *

— We ask for signs — says Uri, — and they give us tricks. Cheap goddamn tricks. Like they make something disppear; then they give it back to us. They bend spoons. They steal parts out of pens. They place hawks in the sky. What kind of men *are* we to dance to this? Are we so fucking hard-up? Is it any wonder I appear like a charlatan? They write my whole routine, and it's Copacabana, nightclub, from beginning to end. — "They have their own ideas, what they want from us, what they need from us, what we need from them. . . . But for us, but for them maybe, the world is not really important. Once in a while. . . . I have the feeling, Andrija, that all we are doing, we are just goddamn slaves for them. They are using us for their own use. They don't care about the world."[6]

— Isn't it just like having a good father? — Andrija protests.

"We don't know them, Andrija, we really don't know them. Andrija, I forget, but you know how far away they are! They are so far that no human mind, not yours, not all the scientists together put in one place, can figure out how far away they are. Different dimensions, future, that's completely way out! That's wild!"[7]

— Still— pleads Andrija, —how can we refuse their gifts?—

Gandalf answers in words so simple they are part of a fairy-tale: "Perilous to us all are the devices of an art deeper than we possess ourselves."[8] For all those aboard the Twentieth Century Unlimited.

For all the Arica intensives, consciousness groups, for all the LSD rebirthing primals, Campground Meetings, Summit Conferences, White and Black Panthers (and Carlos Castaneda bounced from the marketplace to the desert by two native American comedians), have we gotten the message?

"Yes," replies Uri. ". . . . and that is what the little clown keeps telling us: "Listen, man, I am also that—so be careful. I don't want to ruin your life. That's why you must always use your own brain—no matter what Spectra says. Tomorrow I might vanish. Tomorrow you won't have any powers, and we will laugh up here, but you're going to have the dregs."[9] —Perhaps I'll even erase your mind and take away all the clues—.

"Fifty years," they wire.

"What!," Puharich exclaims in dismay. "We are to be left alone for fifty years?"

"YOU ARE ALL ALONE NOW
ALL OF YOU FOR A LONG TIME"[10]

And twenty-five centuries back, Heraclitus wrote: "The lord whose oracle is at Delphi neither speaks nor conceals, but gives signs."[11]

—And what does it mean to you that we know we exist?—
asks Andrija.

Uri answers: "To my sorrow and to my disappointment, I
don't really know."[12]

*   *   *

The next day the psychics invite us to dinner. In a comfortable
living room, over wine, after a discussion of the interior decorating,
they announce wonderful new proofs of their powers, ghosts driven
from the summer cottages of starlets, neutrinos and other rays they
imagine they control. With the paperback on Soviet work in ESP
at their fingertips they predict a century of miracles, one event
after another, removing the cauls off energy and matter. They
will sit beside Generals at the Pentagon.

Their optimism is, in fact, blasphemy. Their own prophecy
that a bomb, set off at Los Alamos, might destroy the very structure
of matter, and them with it, AND ALL OF CREATION ITSELF,
to set it off anyway.

Now their leader stands and addresses us: —If the Russians
get it too— he says —there'll be warfare on the astral, a period
of darkness unprecedented on this planet. It will ignite the Third
World War, battle by mind—.

He takes his seat, a warrior in a business suit, an American
as surely as Bobby Fischer or John Carter, but with a foe more
resourceful than the blowdart Indians of Argentina or the chessmen
of Mars. His commitment is total. He cannot answer humbly, as
the rest of us might:

"I am of another world, the great planet Earth, which re-
volves about our common sun and the next within the orbit of
your Barsoom, which we know as Mars. How I came here I cannot tell you, for I do not know; but here I am, and since my
presence has permitted me to serve Dejah Thoris I am glad that
I am here."[13]

The lights flickering, the steam of the indoors on the open
window, hot and cold and bending in dance; a vision: the city
melting into a brilliant rose garden, with delights more driven than
sugar or natural gas. We see that a world of ethers, a planetary

and yogic world, surrounds, enthralls, and binds, this.

For each of us is used by the gods, as the gods use the masters, differently. When the psychics turn to me — for I have been
silent — and ask my thoughts on the matter, I tell them that all
this business of neutrinos, energies, dowsing, and the like, is secondary because like atomic power and test-tube life, it is an endless
bin of wonders and possibilities, none of which speak to our actual
dilemma, even as technology has not really spoken to the dilemma
that brought it into being. And to their theory about what remains
of the Twentieth Century I tell them: the real issue before us is
HOW WE LIVE.

And they are silent.

I tell them: the real issue is HOW WE LIVE, dragging mares'
tails, wagons, our own human flesh, whatever; underwater, in
outer space, in the super-floating-cities, whether we shoot each
other with bullets, zap with our minds, or thoughtlessly slaughter
the innocent beast; whether we are all psychic or none of us
psychic, whether we come to live on the Moon or abandon the
Moon, and when we are done with all other questions, this alone
will remain.

1973–1975

THIRD WORLD WIPEOUT

from *Martian Homecoming at the All-American Revival Church* and *The Unfinished Business of Doctor Hermes*

Where can Eldridge Cleaver go? He comes back to America he'll be slapped in the can with Patty Hearst and Charles Manson. *Mission: Impossible* and the guerrilla groupies are playing Cuba. In Algeria, it's Superfly-Supernarc, those Heckle and Jeckle lovers. In North Korea, *Combat* has been held over the fifteenth year; *WR: Mysteries of the Organism* has been cancelled. Cleaver's unlikely companion is another fugitive — Dr. Timothy Leary, fleeing the academics, Buddhists, and Feds, talking outer space, life extension, and general ecstasy. The Pope of Dope takes a seat beside the Black Panther boss because no one told either of them they were on the same Third World train. Just as no one told SDS in the sixties that Mao had already signed with Nixon; and while *they* were taking rifle practice behind the cities and sabotaging troop trains, *he* was playing out his option in Peking. If Cleaver decides to hang out in China, he may well meet the next American president, under KGB protection, fleeing the CIA.

It used to be guerrilla armies, men and women in the fields together, harvesting rice and sugar for their brothers and sisters; they were our only alternative to Madison Avenue and the Bomb. Now it's the international drug traffic; spice, dope, and oil; the Marco Polo special; Blackboard Jungle; and 125 to nothing votes in the U.N. (North America abstaining). Tomorrow the vote could be 135 to nothing, or 270 to nothing. Scores which express only that everyone speaks Hopi, or, worse, that everyone reads *The New York Times*. While camera-men run around photographing the century.

The politics of the sixties and seventies never really happened. The Chinese and Africans could smell it from light centuries away. If the Black Panthers and SDS felt jilted by Mao, even that was an overevaluation. Mao never heard of them — because, from that distance, they were indistinguishable from Disneyland or the general democratic hoopla: Rennie Davis awaiting a wave of bliss to engulf *this* world from the Divine Light Mission; Jerry Rubin, after rolfing, gestalt, massage, yoga, sex with a surrogate, talking about how his consciousness is now raised to where he no longer fears pleasure and success. Tom Hayden, campaigning for the Senate with his movie actress wife, would not see it that way. But why shouldn't they all adopt gurus and live in palaces? Why shouldn't they sell their memoirs and live off the proceeds? They earned it. They were the rock stars of our youth. Now they marry Jane Fonda and ask to represent us. They borrow Third World debt from the international money fund. They export baseball and golf.

Hirohito, who engineered the bombing of Pearl Harbor, returns to visit Williamsburg, Virginia, and Disneyland, our honored guest. He is in a trance, but he was in a trance then.

So the Third World disappears back into folk bands playing on mestizo streets. Food Stamps and Poetry in the Schools. General Amin on the podium of the U.N., his sex so weighted down with medals it is hard to tell whether he represents 42nd Street or the Nile. He murders his wives, accuses his ambassador of intercourse with a foreign operative in the Orly Airport toilet; she vanishes; he comes to New York to speak for the oppressed. If the American ambassador complains it is like when the crazies take over the asylum, shouldn't he also remember that this is the role he once assigned to Africa, as if it were a million dollars, when he first filed it under provincial resources during the Sixth Dynasty?

When Amin insists on addressing the Assembly in Ugandan, as when he has four Britishers carry him on a litter, he is closest to a surrealist accuracy. The heavier the rhetoric, the more dra-

matic some totally other plight. You can talk about Pentagon
Papers and secret tapes, but our nation rises and falls, unknown
to the electorate, on the bodies of three dead Martians, kept in
the White House vault, and shown to each new president on his
first day of office. Just to let him know what it's all about. Don't
you see it on his very face still. The compulsive who gives away
his secret by the fervor with which he holds another.

Everyone has their own version of the cultural revolution,
the big shakedown, their own excuse for mass torture. Afterwards,
they can put on a suit and sell out on the open market, African
voodoo-society members led to the shorning as effortlessly as British
bureaucrats. Marxism in the American University is hardly a value;
it's a position to defend, irritably, against the ignorant, like New
Criticism or Plain Truth.

There is no mafia or guerrilla liberation team that does not
conspire across the big gameboard with the imperialists. Although
carcasses are at stake and the enemy is engaged in terrorism against
civilians, both sides have made life ideologically dear, leaving only
the negotiators, as long as they are alive, drinking wine in Paris,
filling their bodies with, in this transitory situation, what make
up the joys of being, even if they feign a spartan existence, to act
out the dilemma history lays on the dispossessed, because the stars
in the sky bring their children into being again and again even
if it is not, as it is for the American Indian, reborn through the
womb of the clan. What is translated into karmic memory and
pure experience must on another level go back to political brink-
manship. The law, international law as well, is there only to assure
that the game is played, not to bind the antagonists. Torture and
genocide are always the last possible moves, from Ethiopia to Cambodia, no matter how gentle the ancient tribes, because politics
always goes to the same extreme as the porn movie, to make a
three-hundred-pound pig fuck a retarded girl.

Cleaver: ". . . . the Cubans had abandoned all aid to liberation movements and this stuff was just like PR. . . . These guys
walked around with cigars sticking out of their beards and guns
around their waists. . . . A lot of women were coming to Cuba. . . .
to get injected with the revolutionary serum by sleeping with a

Cuban. . . . (And) they liked nothing better than meeting these women's fantasies. . . . The final shock came the day I saw Richard Nixon shaking hands with Chairman Mao. When you see Nixon and all that he stands for shaking hands with Mao and all that he supposedly stood for — well, it marks a turning point in history and a personal turning point for me."[1]

*   *   *

Third World Industries swings into overkill — the rock music companies speaking sweetly through their ads like enlightened big brother, trying to sell us their prime time freaks at prime time rates. They are also selling their friendship, their pretence that they speak with our voice. But in this day of chemical suck-off and mind-bend equal to submarine warfare, is it so simple to know who is the dope-dealer, who is the addict, and who is leading us like lambs to the slaughter?

Naropa Institue ads on the mainline. — Come be initiated with the world's hotshit dancers and poets. Imported Buddhist University with resident American sages — . Because they are so much better than that, there is no excuse for it. No excuse.

The victory of the Western World is so much more complete than anyone realizes; these are only its spoils the rest of them are fighting over. The Khmer Republic, selling us their gold coins through a firm in Florida. Iowa grain in the bakeries of Moscow, Russian oil on Interstate 20, outside Des Moines.

Don King, ex-numbers-racketeer, hops out of prison and starts bargaining with dictators, selling them prize fights: Venezuela, Zaire, Malaysia, the Philippines. He couldn't open a pawn shop in Cleveland or a car wash in Helena, but these nations are somewhere else. That's your Third World: exporting Transcendental Meditation, copper, and reggae, importing nuclear reactors, rodeos, fried chicken. "Here he is," announces Ali as his opponent arrives, "the heavyweight champeen of the world, Joe Fraz-ur." Inviting him up on center stage — and the man might as well accept, or give up the whole gig. Pure Louisville Harlem jive, and the kings of Africa and South Sea dictators can't wait to buy it. The big man's now squiring Marcos and his wife, planning to export sugar from Manila to Africa, having put away the gorilla in the thrilla. —A company? Well, if I don't have one, I'll set one right up—.

Despite our obsession with him as hero, Mao is still an obscure figure to us in America; he is at least as duplicit as Don Juan. Our sense of his overwhelming power and ideological purity distracts us from the fact that he is in the same boat as all the rest of us, by the time and planet of his birth. He is neither impregnable nor transhistorical; he is not wise enough or alien enough to be from outer space. He is more trickster coyote than Confucian sage.

And was Nixon the enemy, or did the real enemy put him out of business because he was a bumbler? (Jack Ruby and Lee Harvey Oswald in tandem, Robert Kennedy lying dead on the floor, Sirhan Sirhan holding the gun.) Was Watergate the shake-down or an audience-participation soap opera, a bicentennial morality play to draw our attention off center stage, the Senators likewise? Do we still follow the carrot instead of the stick?

Cleaver: "Tim is an old man and five years in prison is like a death sentence. So when he turns in these people he isn't sing-ing on people he loves; no, he is singing against bastards who he would like to see in the same position. At one point he said that he had been ripped off by the new left, the old left, the sideways left; and he does see it like he was ripped off and, man, we all were."[2]

Who said blood is thicker than spirit? (when the witch-doctor is yet more powerful than the chief). It is their Trojan War, not ours, their revolution, our rhetoric. Any confirmed IRA gunman could be a reactionary banker in London tomorrow. Richard Nixon is a potential Black Panther liaison, a head numbers man. A Maoist agricultural worker in the next life becomes an Idaho farm mag-nate. The Chicago Seven are also the seven oil companies; if they aren't, they will be. If nominated, they will run.

That is why all of them meet so easily as heads of state, from their opposite ideologies. That is why Amin speaks Ugandan in defiance, and Palestinians give their lives in violent self-destructive acts for the cause—to prove to themselves, and the world, that their ideology is somehow more than skin-deep, that it goes to the center of their being, that there is no way, no way, they could be born again as Swiss industrialists or Arkansas Little Leaguers.

Patty Hearst has proven publicly what has been true for us all along. The ascetics, the angry bomb throwers, are also the hedonists, the upholders of the system. They go from strict yoga to loose living; part-time vegetarians, part-time dropouts, part-time capitalists, children of America/Third World revolutionaries, who quit smoking on Sunday TV football or buying California lettuce or hung-up sexuality, for a day, a month, a year, or two.

When Hearst is reclaimed from the SLA, there is a national debate about whether she is a kidnap victim or Tanya the urban guerilla. Do they assume that *she* could supply the answer? Can't she be both? In Cleaver it makes sense. From his dharma center he can either advocate the overthrow of America or praise the American military; he can change from a left wing radical to a patriot, and make it stand. These positions have nothing to do with who Eldridge Cleaver is. — Look — he warns the New Left, — you can be true blue and a rebel dead and all that kind of stuff, but it's only teams, it's like the solidarity of the Green Bay Packers or the Teamsters; it isn't real or anything. It doesn't make the world better or your sex life healthier; it doesn't put you in touch with any human being. And while you're building your castles of outmoded rationality, the real pigs are fucking your women and kicking up your grape orchards — . "The left has really blown itself because we always felt compelled to embrace the opposite extreme. Why should we have allowed Nixon to wrap himself in the American flag? We should have taken it away from that motherfucker. But instead we grabbed the Viet Cong flag. . . ."[3]

And you question Patty Hearst! When the Watergate conspirators become radicals and preachers and write poetry in jail, and preachers become politicians and defense contractors, and H. Howard Hunt's spy novels sit beside those of Raymond Chandler. John Ehrlichman living as a beach bum in Arizona, hanging out with freaks and offering to defend Indian rights? Communist bosses picking out their designer clothes on Fifth Avenue? Indians investing in the world oil market? Psychics running venture-capital firms?

Even as Alger Hiss is readmitted to the bar, the Rosenberg case is reopened. The judgments of one decade are reversed entirely, within the same legal system (the judge not batting an eyelash); they are reversed while, in some basic way, not changing. The fluctuating Harris Poll is first and foremost a measure of hypocrisy, but a hypocrisy so basic it is a wonder we tried to make a world in defiance of it.

In Patty Hearst the contradiction is deeper than her life. The ideologies of the sixties and seventies blow over her as various attractive winds in which she seems to find her courage, her sexuality, her identity. From the beginning, she was an actress in a movie, and for seventeen months she played another part. She lived it and could have died it, and it would have made her no more or less a revolutionary, no more or less than if she allows her parents' defense lawyers to talk her out of the whole thing.

We have gone past ideology and revolution; the stuff we are in is deep. The Madison Avenue good guys, with their baroque human characteristics, do not understand the enemy. It is not that he does not care for the people (he adores them); it is that he is made of imaginary numbers, sustained by a computer operation on a planetary scale that would make Fort Knox look like Cherokee archaeology.

The Zionists strike from an explicit world of tanks and jets this world has all but abandoned, acting out a World War II movie of courage and strategic daring, because they were the helpless chaff of that war. They are the new secular materialists, despoilers of the Qabala. The Palestinians are left with one alternative: Terrorists strike not at the enemy but at political meaning itself, at the world market that excludes them by mere convenience, at the planes and boats carrying out seemingly neutral daily commerce. Because, they proclaim, it is the dead-weight background of the world that itself must be challenged, that contains their death wish. The so-called falsification of meaning goes beyond our fondest dreams, thus fulfills our deepest fears.

*   *   *

An announcement is made on the networks: a foreign galaxy is being drawn into this one. The Earth will be annihilated. People are outraged. They call up and demand the government to do something about it. Build a wall. Explode an atomic bomb.

When Orson Welles staged his invasion, thousands of people called the Pentagon offering to enlist to fight against the Martians. But this, of course, is not the problem; the problem is that we are led to create and imagine such possibilities to express the dilemma we find ourselves in. We are so exhaustive in our explorations and investigations, in our accumulation of paper profit, that it is no wonder we are weak as hell in cosmology, weak in the link between our status as sentient beings and the systems we invent and give a life of their own.

"The Voice of my Higher Self said unto me: Let me enter the Path of Darkness and, peradventure, there shall I find the Light. I am the only Being in an Abyss of Darkness; from an Abyss of Darkness came I forth ere my birth, from the Silence of a Primal Sleep." (Aleister Crowley).

All we do is dwarfed by the backdrop of time and emergence, and even by the memory and flowingness of our thoughts. It is no wonder that problems which arise first in industry and agriculture are metaphysical problems, are, in fact, the same problems that exist in wards of schizophrenics, in definitions of quasars, in the inability to reverse degradation in the urban slums. The big agricultural combines and multi-farm companies do not exist in some vacuum from our so-called radical entrenchment. They exist hand-in-glove with the record companies, the AMA, the philosophy and literature departments of the University, *The Washington Post, Time Magazine*, and so on. Modern medicine, like the oil industry, is unprincipled from the start. Not unethical but unprincipled. Without any theory of medicinal agent or cure. For us to waste our focus on standard AMA malpractice, chemotherapy, incompetent treatment, elitist profit-greedy health plans, is like blaming the Arabs for the oil crisis. Doctors are slightly more skilled auto mechanics, and we sit at the end of a rat-monkey-prisoner experimental chain, antibiotic, hence anti-life. How could their ethics be any better when this is the flaw they are hiding?

The war is clearly between the ecologists and the psychics,

and it is not a happy one. The rules are: who will destroy us first. It is not a war of power and territory, but of moralism. The ecologists want to cut the actual living base from under us because of what we have done to nature. The psychics conjure to bring on earthquakes and astral war because we have abandoned their gods.

— Wait — you say. — You've got it wrong. It's not that they want to do it *to* us; they want to warn us; they want us to prepare ourselves; they want to prevent it — .

But it doesn't matter. As in Aesop's fable, the Messenger must be killed for the message by which he has made his living. Those who discover the apocalypse are, strangely, its handmaidens; in their commitment to computers, management science, and behaviorism they remain the final and most compelling resistance of the race to change. They want to go on stolid or be blown away.

Eco-holocaust, they cry. No, first earthquake, scream the prophets. War in the Holy Land.

And they sit there like wrestling coaches, demanding the impossible. Get your shit together or it's all over. To say nothing of your neighbors' shit if your own were down to error zero. If it won't be the impossible, then you lose. You're a ten touchdown underdog, but go out and beat State, Coach says. It's impossible, right? But then it's always been impossible. And that's the Islamic sword.

* * *

It is probably a good thing that people are splitting up and marriages ending obscurely. It is a good thing insofar as people are breaking off a rigid unfelt form. But there is another side: Perhaps it wasn't marriage they were once committed to. They seemed to choose marriage, but it was automatic. They were really saying: We want to live here, we want to be one of you. Now they no longer want to put their energy in trust, even as they no longer want to put their money in stocks or city bonds. They are afraid they will be left with nothing; they are afraid they will put in their whole life (their whole life) working for a company that goes bankrupt and is unable to pay their pension.

As the prophets announce the end is near, hundreds are slowly stampeded from the city. They go to the country; they build or buy houses; they pick up local social service jobs; they form co-ops and put up preparatory windmills. And if the end does not come soon enough, some must return to the city for refresher courses in Silva Mind Control. Those who originate in the vagueness of the city suffer dislocation among the concrete objects of the farm, despite their longing for substance; they find that after the first years they cannot put in a planting, cannot even keep together their families and friends.

It grows in the guise of a positive ideology, liberation and sexuality, personal development, but it is more profoundly an implement of fear and darkness, as people flee coherence, as they lose their confidence in a center, as they are refugees, in the dream of liberation and ecstasy, from a broken society and live alone because they don't trust the banks, because everyone is an American, a sexist, an imperialist, even themselves.

So we sit in a world which is not the world. It comes to us as global anxiety, bizarre migrations, sudden violence in Greece, Lebanon, Portugal, Cambodia, Dakota. Like the Romans we have the illusion that nothing like the Middle Ages can follow us, because nothing like them preceded our reign. We fondly remember Rome. We are but her pale shadow, and we can fall from power only more sharply and precipitously. We are Rome that has not fallen: the glory all the thinner, all the more manufactured and ephemeral for our greater distance from the source.

This whole human world was once an infinite point — tribal man. The first history of the planet can be seen as the movement East against the movement West; their collision is the extermination of the Indians — who left Cro-Magnon man in the caves of France 50,000 years ago and rode east across Russia. China and America meet again on the Western Ocean, the declivity the edge of which is Russia and England. India, for being Indo-European, belongs to the West, at the level of Ireland out in the Atlantic. Japan striking at Pearl Harbor was a memory trace, a reminder of debts and obligations buried in global consciousness. The Peruvian Indians were victims, victims of the Inca first, the half-breed generals last. The Montagnais were used in both Vietnamese armies. The Basques launch their attacks from the old Atlantic. There are no non-combatants, but there are those whose stillness measures the whisper.

We live still in a Roman world. We retain, in archetype and urban structure, if not in coins and petroglyphs, the kin ties of Neolithic tribes, whose hierarchies bound the world in an equality no system has since restored. The proletariat is a joke beside the billions of acres of independent gatherers and smalltime farmers of the prior Earth. And our cities are now like cartoons amid the permafrost and coal-beds, the termitaries and wild birds. We are the last and most costumed guests at the Roman party. But we act like the saviors of mankind.

God knows, it is not our *call to arms* that exonerates us in the ledgers of a Third World creation myth; it is how humanely we do the number of being us while they do the number of being them. The liberals are still benighted enough to think we can help them by the positive power of our beliefs, or even our preference to be them, *even* our preference to help them before we help us. *They* know better. They simply want our cars and houses and mass-produced gadgets, our supermarkets and nightclubs. They don't want our piety or after-dinner globalism.

Because we do not know enough. Because we will never know enough. And our attempts to seal this period of history with the same finality with which we have pretended to seal the Franks and Huns are little more than big city bravado.

We lie in oblivion and whether what will cover us is Chinese or not will not matter. We sit in a hollow grandstand, and when it disappears it will take with it not just the mask of the falling metropolis but the shadows of our narcissistic gods.

*   *   *

We don't want it.

If we wanted it, we could have it. (Just like if we wanted marriage, we could have it; it we wanted utopia. . . .)

Why R.B. Fuller says: that, or oblivion — not realizing that he as well as us are the product of a choice made long ago.

1973–1975

DEEP NUMERICAL MUSIC

from *The Slag of Creation*

Those who lived in beehives are gone, and the wind of centuries blows dirt against their stone relics. We are dolls, doll-like fragments of their incomplete design, winding roads that evade the object, yet return again and again. History is not enough. "After this life there's another life," my child says decidedly, but he has too much confidence to see the dismantling that goes on all around us, that destroys nothing, that parts no thread. The nut we pretend to crack plants only further trees in the distances, and as the forest becomes deeper and orientation more vast, we wonder how it ever seemed simple, how we ever imagined we could tame it as a garden. When I call Morgan on the phone, the sound, he tells me, is like the Buddhist gong, in the center of meditation, calling him back mercifully into the world of things. The bats at twilight, irregular in the windows, wear bats. Rigel, Capella, Aldebaran. Faint Pleiades. There is no fresco dripping, there are no masks; the form seals even before the blue glaze reflects it, the circle pouring from the hidden wheel.

We live now between a supercivilization that sprays the cosmos with messages and prophecies, blueprints of a golden age, and a Buddhist revision in which we renounce not only the outer space gambit but our own Rosicrucian city. The intergalactic beam wheels through creation, spreading seeds and notes that translate

47

as possibilities in any particular world. Atlantis merging with
Andromeda. But if we stir to the panpipes of these Saturnian magi
or trust Clarke's overlord-guides and the possibility of "childhood's
end," these are desperate acts, our priests tell us. For even if they
have the machinery to build cities as large as the Sun, to accommodate our restlessness till eternity, they cannot pull us, when body
and soul mean to divide, from the abyss. And surely they do not
operate beyond it.

Their music is everywhere, promising us life, tempting us to
be what we think we are, to use our materials creatively, despite
their obvious incapacity before the task. They do not deny death,
but their spacecrafts, operating at the speed of light and archetype,
turn time into cream, and drink it, as the fuel. They litter our
laboratories and telescopes joyfully, trying to initiate us by the
sphinx of cosmic cities. Yet how's that different, asks Gary Snyder,
from the whole trip of America to the original Indians?

Technology is not the real prize of the West. It couldn't be,
not with its reliance on cheap underground energy and its ram-
shackle agricultures and medicine. It just doesn't work. Its clear
sight, its vision of a furnace sun, is a darkness most of creation
will never know. The real prize is a methodology we do not even
begin to understand—a methodology that creates while it destroys,
which, at the same time it makes the planet toxic and unfit, draws
more and more fantastic machines from its belly.

The enigma of our age is that we cannot separate the parts
that work from the parts that do not. We have made a machinery
that cannot hold even itself together. We have built a beautiful
and sacred factory and given it nothing real to process; its fleet
lies abandoned and ignored. So they fill its trucks not even with
dung and waste, but with each other, and drive them into gullies
where they disintegrate and are washed away. And what they
preserve, in their tinhorn pride, is a dime a dozen in this galaxy.
A cheap two-bit robot breeding cancer and insanity. We could
do so much better with what we have. We don't really know what
we have. And even then, whispers the other voice, does it matter?, do we really care?, knowing how all this is going to end.
Yet if we really don't care, it is going to be more than the Bud-

dha's stunning reversal. This is all going to disappear with a rapidity to make us wonder who ever went through the trouble in the first place.

Sam warns me not to forget the music we heard in college. He came to Vermont for a rest in the woods, but he's got those Ecology Conference Apocalypse blues. "Who wants to play the piano if the whole thing's coming down." Because that's all they talk about now. Their radical anger is vented in their hopes that the war-makers are going to put under their own machine.

What is the music?, I ask him. It's a refinement, he says. A refinement of what, I don't know. It is subtle. It comes from faraway. There is no archetypal melody. It's all built up, tune and association, from what's here. But still, he says, I feel as though I am transferring notes of a great code; I *am* helping even if I'm not building windmills. I am bringing things into existence at the lowest denominator. So low no one could possibly recognize them. For years, maybe centuries, to come. But how else are they to get here? Surely not by the literal discussion of community and societal rebuilding or by hi-tech elaborations upon the gargantuan and everpresent machinery. There are things we don't even know to know about. We can't begin to want them. We can't imagine where they come from. Their perspective sits beyond a point beyond Pluto, *at* a point. They spray the androgyne as fertilely as tassels dust the wombs of corn. We must selflessly and subtly serve as their agents. Wherever it comes from, do not look to the visible cosmos. Do not look for friendly astronauts. The sky is but a metaphor, accurate in its astronomical and astrological boundaries, for the source. If we don't allow them to find us, if we don't lay ourselves bare at every stage of the way, even our mistakes, our evasions, then speculation is for naught. You don't have to play it on radio-telescope vibes and beam it at Cassiopeia to make contact with the Other. The discovery of *our* muffled drum is so much more important, Mahler, Schoenberg, Cage, than *their* discovery of us.

We are writing alchemical instructions, in our confusion of amulets, techniques, and texts. This is the famous historical confusion;

the alchemists were not the only ones who mixed molecules, gods, psychic processes, and technology. Our contribution to solving the riddles *is* the riddles, even as the Mediaeval attempts upon Neo-platonic riddles upon Egyptian riddles upon the Palaeolithic heritage upon the origin of language in call systems upon the mute wild planet upon the zone of moons and suns. What is lost we will never know. What we maintain is the basic bare continuity of the present, even whose attack upon hermeticism is a hermetic text.

1974

VISION QUEST

I awake from a nap brought on by a headache. I awake suddenly on the edge of my being, the abruptness so much more certain than the headache. The headache is gone. But as if its throb had broken, in unconsciousness, through the dreaming mind, to the forgotten beginning. And two rocks now stand, the agency having passed, stand separated. Their gap is the abyss.

If light moves through eternity undriven, what impels it, particle by particle, what gets it there?

Life makes itself familiar; it insists on me. I am the child watching the street from a city window. I stand in the long hallway as my stepfather opens the black door. There is a blue flower imposed on a thousand such blues, going back forever, and the blueness of the sky; there are golden daisies, in a space so immense, so young and splendid, its sheer fabric wrapped in my fabric overwhelms language and philosophy.

I awake from my nap with the connection broken. Eating an orange now will not restore it. I have been here, as long as I can remember. When I can no longer remember, I am as one splash in a frogpond, which ends. And the entirety of summer twilight hangs over it, the mosquitoes, before me as after me. You say the only trouble with dying is you do it for such a long time. But it also takes an awful long time to get born. Rocks on either side. And the headache, having dissolved, sucks an orange. The

51

giant crumbles into words and events.

You say death stalks me. Yes. By now there is no other explanation possible. But I do not know it as death. It is all the things I do which stalk me: my breakfast, my friendship, the persistent light of the sun I see through these stones called eyes.

The thing I call death does not stalk me. And this leaves the illusion I do not fear death. So that when I awake from the nap, something else is there, bigger than I am, like a wind that could lift me away. Even that is not quite death. The word death is a fraud, a hedge. My experience of eternity is my body itself, because every fiber courses with fluid, every drop of fluid touches thought, every thought returns to complete the circle. There is nothing bigger than me, but my congruence, reimposed, is as big and as devastating as any annihilation. I am suspended, like Robert Fludd's angel, between amber and midnight stars.

Death comes as a strange notion only. All this, will not be forever. Forever. And the smell hangs there, the smell of anything, of meat cooking behind another house. It alone marks the spot. You could dismantle reality image by image, and it would not break the connection. We live all our lives knowing the connection will be broken.

The astral body is terrifying and the soul is terrifying. And they solve nothing, either for the occultist who believes in them or the scientist who takes for granted that they do not exist. Belief is not the body. The body knows, and the mind's wish to join the body and belief in a pure monogamy is one way not to live at all. Nothing is true: the ocean takes care of that in its bed of sand.

If the soul does not exist, it is terrifying.

If it does exist, it is terrifying.

The full meaning is detoured. That I go on as something else, adds nothing to that. The spiritual does not interfere with the world it has created. And that alone makes it the spiritual.

Wanting to live too much is the joke we play on ourselves. Penny wise, pound foolish, we stand determinedly on the side of life. A city in sunlight stands for us, there, in our place. And we inhabit it. Sparsely and intimately. Its stones too are under erosion by light and wind.

Certain acts seem to us savage. Even to the most sympathetic anthropologist the North American Indian vision-quest is brutal. He records its having happened, but he is grateful that he does not have to undergo it. He records it for study, and we enter on his side of the skēnē, with the illusion this is what they do, not what we do:

A young boy, with only the minimum tools of survival, goes into the forest. We accept that animal death and death by starvation are real possibilities for him; *he* knows that spirit death also pursues him. He must seek not only food and drink, but, even as he flees animals for whom he is prey, he must find supernatural beings who may or may not exist.

Our savage mind is caught in a dilemma, which is also its bloody bondage to our animal heart. Do I want to live?, it asks. No. is the answer. The animals guard meaning in a kingdom all to itself, they alone. And the rest has that funny shadowy sense that blows away, and us in the center, us, not the mind.

The first answer must be no. This is neither sentimental nor existential; it is the priority. The Indian boy faces this on his quest. The wish not to live is greater than the wish to live. The choice to live must be made then and there, consciously, as an animal choice. The bear comes out of the wilderness and out of the mist, fleshy and bloody and fibrous, yes, even congruent, and not as a symbol for something and something else. It connects the mind to the heart. No more false success to buy off life. No more trinkets and record albums and dope. No more filling the void with desire for the maidens. All these things are dropped. Later, all these things come back.

We are not savages and we are not civilized. We fill the city with time that buys off our precious time, while sun fills the city too. We collectivize our suicide, placing first our birth in the false security of blankness, as if in the brazen secularity of the hospital we came into this world fully-formed, why then crying of a darker and bloodier place? We nurse out chemical deaths, be they head or body, body nonetheless. My brother did it in a mental hospital, drugged and mindfucked. Add it up, one way or another, it comes out to about ten or eleven years of his life. If we had been a civilized family, like those who lived here before our ancestors brought their broken Rosicrucian dreams, he could have taken it into the star-clear night. He could have stalked, in the vastness of this nebula formation, the traces of his own formation. It could have been a song.

We have reduced our effectuality. We make the decision to live again and again and again, and still have it to make. The angst of the West arises solely in this condition. We have access to no more profound tragedy or deity. The best of our modern novels take their beauty and longing from beneath this arch. Glorious it is. Vaster and more devious than any Indian life. But it stands on a pebble. It is as though, being unable to complete the first step, we are now up somewhere in the hundred thousands plus. And have forgotten. Because only one is missing. That it is the first one. And awake at moments startled and clinging to a raft while winds of unusual velocity threaten to separate meaning from its coil.

We are on a petroleum high, taken long and slow, and hard and deep, and not in the blood. Our paranoia is a petroleum downer. Nothing but these various vehicles and chariots could take us through the unexperienced landscape at a proper speed. By now, this late in the game, everything got here, even the seeds of the plants, on the funeral pyres of the ancestors. The fluid of life is unbroken. And it is not our life.

We admire the vision-quest, but it holds no romanticism for its remaining practitioners. Even as we destroy — when we find — the thousands of possible worlds around them, they will never now inhabit, they contemplate the eternal beginning.

1975

THE BRAZILIAN MASTER
IN BERKELEY

Capoeira is virtually unknown in the United States. Even most educated people would be surprised to learn that it is a native Brazilian art with roots in Africa. Those who know of it superficially might picture a combination of Brazilian music and folk theatre, but *Capoeira* is a preliterate system of knowledge and philosophy that has also trained some of the most deadly warriors our species has known.

The roots of *Capoeira* disappear into the chaos of sixteenth-century Brazil. Clearly, major aspects of *Capoeira* are African, arising from the music, dance, folklore, and warfare of various Yoruba, Malé, Dahomean, Bantu, and Hausa refugees. But *Capoeira* itself represents a combination of regional traditions syncretized by the wild forces of early pan-Brazilian culture. Even the etymology of the name is in doubt, having alternative derivations from a Guarani Indian term for cut wood and a Portuguese folk name for a particularly aggressive male species of bird.

By the time a written history of *Capoeira* appears in the eighteenth century, it is already a popular form of street-fighting, and the *Capoeirista* is a well-known trickster-warrior in Brazilian folklore, with aspects of both the thief and the early guerrilla freedom-fighter. Over the years it has been so associated with outlaws and the lower classes in Brazil that it has had difficulty gaining legality, let alone respect. Today it is regarded as a kind

of rough ethnic sport and back alley training, though it has gained
some stature in the last ten years and there are several *Capoeira*
gyms and schools in major cities with government sanction.

I first heard of *Capoeira* in the spring of 1982. I was editing
a book by a retired CIA agent writing under the name of John
Gilbey.[1] "Gilbey" had taken advantage of his global travel op-
portunities to seek obscure fighters of ancient internal traditions.
These included an Icelandic master of *Fotan*, an ancient system
of crushing rocks by paraphysical methods; a Hawaiian Kahuna
adept in *Lua* (a body-twisting voodoo); and various other gurus,
warriors, charlatans, and shamans, with Gilbey leaving the reader
to decide the authenticity of each practice. There was also a
Capoeirista. For background on him Gilbey reviewed and sum-
marized the conflicting Brazilian literature on this subject, and
I will further condense some of his main themes:

In Africa, *Capoeira* was a psychic and religious dance, and
the Bantus in particular continued to practice it in Brazil, blend-
ing it with other ceremonies and adapting it to severe slave conditions. At this stage the practice of *Capoeira* generated a deep
and powerful trance, the skilled practitioner entering into other
realms of being. This trance was a source of both enlightenment
and relief. As in the Plains Indian vision-quest, lessons and techniques were passed on by spirits and allies in other dimensions of
consciousness. One of these was a method of combat while shackled.
The *Capoeiristas* learned to fight with their legs and heads; to feint
and tumble and spin in complex maneuvers; and to hide sharp
objects between their toes, in their specially-combed kinky hair,
and at other unexpected parts of their persons. Blended with witchcraft, voodoo, and chanting, and embodied in a series of initiation
rites, *Capoeira* fighting blossomed and spread among the kingdoms
of escaped slaves in the interior of Brazil; when it returned from
the jungles in the nineteenth century it was in the form of self-
made armies of *Capoeiristas* invading and plundering the cities.
More than 15,000 invaded Rio, and in 1808 a special military police
was founded, with one of its missions to quell the *Capoeiristas*.
At its head was Major Miguel Nunes Vidigal, a traitor *Capoeirista*
who enjoyed dreaming up special tortures for his former comrades,

the most frightening of which can be translated, ambiguously, as "The Shrimp Supper."

Although *Capoeiristas* later allied with various governments of Brazil to fight against Paraguay and to expel German and Irish mercenaries, enough of them were considered bandits and pranksters that laws were passed forbidding the practice and teaching of the art. In 1932, *Capoeira* took a new course: the generally-recognized master of the skill, Mestre Bimba, opened an academy in Bahia. It was later recognized by the Office of Education and Public Assistance in 1937. Mestre Bimba incorporated the many styles and moves of *Capoeira* into a single set of movements and a formal practice with levels of development.

Gilbey's account left me curious, but I pictured *Capoeira* as something between other-galaxy science fiction and a scene from an old black-and-white movie, and I did not expect to hear of it again. Perhaps it was even one of Gilbey's tall tales. But only a few weeks later, in one of those curious coincidences, the decades and miles that apparently separated any American from *Capoeira* vanished on an afternoon in Berkeley. Richard Heckler, an acquaintance well-known for his use of martial techniques in therapy, told me out of the blue that he had been studying *Capoeira* with one of the real masters. Remembering Gilbey, I said something about African slaves in Brazil. "That's it," he nodded in astonishment.

Bira Almeida, known back home as Mestre Acordeon — one of only ten "mestres" certified by Mestre Bimba — had begun teaching in the Bay Area. It turned out that he was also assembling a book on *Capoeira* and needed advice on editing and publishing. I took his phone number and called him. He was witty and charming with his South American accent, and we set up a meeting for later that week before his class at Julius Baker's Tae Kwon-Do Studio in downtown Berkeley.

As I tentatively entered Julius Baker's, I was looking at a class of Afro-Americans practicing hard jabs in unison as they shouted. But almost at once the class ended, and I began asking around for Bira Almeida. No one seemed to know him, and I was told mainly to stay off the mat. The next class was forming all the way on the other side of the mat by the dressing rooms. I could only hope that it was Bira's and that he would remember and look for me.

None of the people in the group seemed quite right for an occult master from Brazil, but when he entered late, he was unmistakable. A tall solidly-built Euro-Brazilian in his late thirties, he moved with bouyant energy and spread an immediate playful jive with calls in English and Portuguese and slaps and pats. In thinking later how to describe him, three very different people came to mind: Fidel Castro for the Latin charisma and quixotic power; but also Don Juan Matus, the Yaqui shaman, for the feeling of wizardry about him, though none of us have seen that one; then there was clearly a bit of Clark Kent about him too, his glasses and briefcase before he changed into the costume of his art.

He addressed his students for ten minutes during which I felt only once that maybe he might have met my eyes long enough to acknowledge me. Just as I was about to give up hope and sit down and watch the class, he broke off, came directly over, introduced himself, and led me into the studio's small office. He patted his briefcase and said in his accented English, "The World *Capoeira* Association, right here."

For fifteen minutes he outlined his project and told me of the difficulties he had encountered. Only at the end, as he was leaving to return to the mat, did he hand me, almost as an afterthought, a copy of his work, suggesting that I look it over and then leave it in the office. Following him out, I found my spot on the bench while still turning through the pages. I began reading at a random spot:

"Mestre Bimba said *Capoeira* is treachery. Long live he who held my hands and showed me how to be in time with the motion. *Capoeira* is also an art one plays anywhere, under any condition, even when in an unbalanced situation. Wherever you are must be the right place to be. And for me, the place is now. So it doesn't matter if some people think I am a fool, crazy, or even presumptuous."

This was no ordinary manuscript. Even as I realized that, a chant exploded and engulfed the room. My condition was transformed. I looked up to see spontaneous theatre—some twenty-five Hispanics, Afros, Euros, surfer and hippie types together with ordinary workers, fat and skinny, old and young, more women than men, many of them dressed in Brazilian costumes and wearing circular *Capoeira Bahia* insignias, several playing *berimbaus*, tall bow-shaped basses strung with tire-cords—others working rattles and drums. They sprang into a circle with Bira at the head; they were opening class with a prayer: "Ie A Capoeira!"

Only later did I realize that all the possibilities I had intuited were present in that moment. And all I could think was: "Wait till they see *this*." I wasn't even sure whom I meant. I guess I meant, "Wait till the rest of the country sees this next wave to come out of California." I looked down at the manuscript:

"I want to see *Capoeira* spread all over the world and my old city of Bahia, *Capoeira*'s main fortress for so long, respected as its sanctuary. I want to see as many people playing *Capoeira* as there are grains of sand on the beach of Amaralina. I want to see the son of the son of my son cutting the space of life in *rabo de arraia*, *mortal*, and fantastic *Capoeira* movements. I want to see you facing the growth of yourself playing *Capoeira*, comfortable and accepted into any *roda*."

The students were now leaping, turning cartwheels over each other, spinning, tumbling, walking on their hands. Top and bottom of their bodies reversed as they moved in graceful circles so swift it seemed impossible they could continue to dodge each other. It was *t'ai chi*; it was *reggae*, it was *West Side Story*, it was *Tristes Tropiques*, it was Gurdjieff in France. I was watching the first wave of the South American invasion, and I saw the ashes of Jonestown and the SLA transformed into a healing dance.

During the next several months I viewed the many faces of *Capoeira* in the Bay Area: Bira was organizing classes for children in the Mission Cultural Center in San Francisco, advising their parents; he was performing with his students in the center of a park in Richmond, pairs of men and women shaking hands, jumping into a circle, and then seeming to fly past one another like acrobats while astonished on-lookers stopped to watch; a few weeks later at a Brazilian-party fund-raiser at the University of California in Berkeley, with the *berimbau* suddenly interrupting the samba, a troupe of exotically-costumed and bare-chested *Capoeiristas* hurtled about the room. A month later, before several hundred mainly singles in a Saturday audience at the Jewish Community Center in San Francisco, Bira was simply a Latin balladeer playing electric guitar, and presenting his own contemporary originals amidst the Bossa Nova, samba, and Batucada. After that, his show picked up with a variety of Brazilian *Carnaval* dances and a brief drama in which a group of fishermen hauled in a costumed "fish" with a complex net while Bira sang a folk ballad backed by his Corpo Santo band. The fish was actually doing a modified *Capoeira* as he crawled along the floor behind the net. As the song ended, the net was abandoned, and the participants became men and women at a village market. Two men argued over a woman, and in a few seconds, *Capoeira* flared up — men, women, and children forming a circle, coming out in pairs to "play," Bira now with *berimbau* in hand, Corpo Santo chanting in the background. A roller-skater with Rastafarian hair challenged the *Capoeiristas* with a sparking cigarette lighter; then he and they chased and dodged each other like clowns but in *Capoeira* movements.

Another time I asked Bira what his goals are. Why did he leave Brazil? Why California? What will become of *Capoeira* in the United States? Does he intend mainly performances or serious study?

"*Capoeira* could not grow in Brazil," he tells me. "It's a developing country, and they think everything good comes from the outside. So they prefer karate and judo. *Capoeira* is despised in middle class circles because they associate it with poor black and mulatto culture. Too many *Capoeiristas* just want to fight and learn martial techniques of any kind. The tradition is lost. In the United States there is the possibility that *Capoeira* could develop and change. Then it will come to Brazil in the only acceptable way: as a Yankee import." He laughs. "They'll say, 'If the Americans do it, maybe there is something to it.' Others will complain, 'There, Bira has gone and taken our Brazilian thing and given it to the Americans.'"

The evolution of *Capoeira* suggests Bira's own development

as a *Capoeirista*. He describes the stages:

"In the first level, the student plays without knowing what is happening. He is lost in space. He sees nothing. Not only do the movements of his opponent seem to materialize by magic, but his own movements are beyond his control. I call this stage 'Playing in the Dark.'"

After this, the student gains a primitive sense of the rhythm and movements, and this is called 'Playing in the Water.' It is followed by a sharp physical mastery when the whole form seems marvellously revealed and everything is possible.

"I reached this stage of 'Playing in the Light' many years ago, training so intensely that I would lose eight pounds each session. I was a fighting machine, challenging my own limits, other *Capoeiristas*, and martial artists of other styles."

This is the highest stage of *Capoeira* today, as Bira sees it, and the reason he has brought it to America — so that Americans will help develop the inner art, and *Capoeira* will come to experience its own depths.

"After four years 'Playing in the Light' I reached my limits and went into a depression. I had such good physical skills and such a strong attitude that I could not easily find challenging opponents. I had no motivation to train for so little possibility of physical and technical improvement. I felt stuck, as if I were facing a large stone wall. I could not see anything more in *Capoeira* for me. So I went to business school and decided to outfit myself in a suit. I graduated four years later, got married, moved to Sao Paolo, and worked in a big company."

He went three years without training or even hearing a *berimbau*. Then he awoke one morning back in Bahia and felt a transformation. The day was filled with light and breeze, and he was inspired by his roots. He felt *Capoeira* in himself and understood that he had missed. He went back into hard training and explored a whole new dimension of the art and his own being.

"I was then able to learn how to play in the fourth level which I call 'Playing with the Crystal Ball.' I didn't care anymore about my strengths, skills, speed, or any other physical aspect. I simply began trying to read the opponent's mind, and set myself in the right place at the right moment."

At this point he understood he should leave Brazil. In order to progress further, he had to translate *Capoeira* into a larger frame, to hear the *berimbau* in the context of the universal rhythm of life. He studied music, wrote plays, explored all different aspects of the tradition.

"Then I reached the last level which I call 'Playing with the Mind.' The opponent must do what your mind silently orders him to do. Such control has no other purpose than to help your opponent, even your enemy, to evolve and to reach a universal harmony through the *Capoeira* way. There is a rhythm to life and to the universe. In doing *Capoeira*, you can play to find it, to attune to it. As long as you are true to this rhythm, you cannot fight a false fight. The rhythm is joyful and gay; it is filled with life's imbalances, but it transforms them. It takes the unpredictability of the world and allows you to move *on* it."

The transformation of *Capoeira* into an art and a means of self-knowledge has been gradual, with Bira Almeida its first spokesman, but the seeds were no doubt there at the beginning. If *Capoeira* had not first confronted bodily freedom from the perspective of the despair of the slaves and tried to ask, 'Why has creation done this to me?', it would not be able to ask questions now about the basic nature of freedom and alienation in the modern world. If it did not test the possibility of total wildness and unrestrained physical power in a young lawless country, only to be subdued by the violence of the reaction, then it would not confront in us the feeling of danger that is present simply in being alive, it would not be able to transform violence into philosophy.

The first practitioners felt that the gods spoke through *Capoeira*, but they needed immediate power far more than an understanding of nature. Perhaps they intuited the other dimensions; certainly they transmitted an art which contained them. *Capoeira* may have started as blind warfare, but it developed a spirit and a soul, and, as importantly, a mode of inquiry whose potential is just now being tapped.

Angry people want to learn to fight in order to maim and to kill; the martial arts do not deny such teaching. But the true internal art turns the anger and alienation back on them and teaches them to recognize the heartbeat and breath of all life's peril in themselves. *Capoeira*, through its unique rhythms, music, and traditions, has the possibility of transforming a small amount of the violence in this country — not a lot, but enough perhaps to make a difference in some people's lives.

One woman explains that *Capoeira* has taught her to move down the street with awareness of all that is happening, to understand threats before they occur and thus to avoid them. She says:

"*Capoeira* is a mirror in which I stand before God and everybody. The reflection casts back my image, brilliantly, magnifying my weaknesses, my limits, and my frustrations. When I played with someone whose energy was totally into themselves and not concerned about me at all, I had to keep playing. I somehow had to find a way to flow in that situation. *Capoeira*, in giving me a mirror image, has forced me to see what I am, and to soften and blend my intensity into a flow which will allow me to grow."

Bira describes the almost inexpressible feeling:

"Many times I would spend hours playing the *berimbau* alone, letting myself travel deep inside my soul, discovering different shapes of my spirit, my weakness, my strength, the consciousness of being alive and in tune with the universe. I played *Capoeira* in the dark of the night on the soft sand of Bahia's beach. Soon I was not able to hear the *berimbau* anymore; I began to feel the sound everywhere, reflecting on the water, on the clouds, on the edge of the earth, resonating inside my body, vibrating in each portion of me. In those moments I felt the full dimension of the *Capoeira* music, the color of its sound. The *berimbau* can pacify the soul when played in melancholy solos; the rhythm is black and strong, a deep and powerful pulse that reaches the heart. It inundates mind, space, and time with the intensity of an ocean tide. The dense aura that emanates from the single musical bow slowly envelops you. Without your realizing it, the powerful magic of the *berimbau* has tamed your soul."

"So you're the philosopher of *Capoeira*," I tell him.

"Not as an ego thing, though," he says, "not like a guru or god. They would laugh in Brazil to hear that Bira is conducting a spiritual study of *Capoeira*. It cannot be put into words anyway. I will simply make it possible for other people to experience parts of this universe that I have been in."

Later he adds, "At the moment you are fighting, your opponent becomes yourself. You confront your fears, your strength and weakness, your life itself. You do this without involving anybody besides your opponent and you. I have been involved in thousands of fights in my life, so I know what it is to feel this kind of thing inside. You know you must win. But to win means to win with yourself. . . . *Capoeira* is like a mirror in which you look at yourself before you wash your face in the morning. You see yourself simply the way that you are and you are there by yourself and yourself alone."

1983

THE RETURN
OF THE WARRIOR

a review of *The Karate Kid*

Western Culture has been slow to respond to the concept of the martial arts as spiritual development or therapy. We have thrown ourselves (individually and collectively) into big and little fights without any sense that the consequences go beyond victory and defeat. We behave as though the winner wins absolutely and the loser is vanquished, and that these are the full range of possibilities. In truth, winner and loser are both changed by a fight in ways that have little to do with stereotyped notions of victory and defeat; they each internalize the confrontation, and its teaching stays with them. The death of the loser does not negate this karma, for not even the victor survives forever. Winners and losers are engaged in a joint process of change to which they each give energy, and the result of their engagement transcends the instantaneous decision of the battlefield (which is merely its external face).

The United States and Europe won on the battlefield in World War II, but Japan and Germany (the supposed losers) were transformed in ways that gave them economic power over the victors. On the other hand, all the winners of that war have borne serious scars of victory. Certainly the State of Israel has paid a steepening spiritual and economic price for each successive triumph in its cycle of Middle Eastern wars.

We are all on this world and in this embodiment together,

65

so events cannot sever our relationships, only alter them. The real consequences of wars unfold for decades, if not centuries and millennia afterwards. It is more than coincidence that the winners are often hardened and trapped by the misleading denouement of their victories while the losers are reborn with new powers.

There is no real "us" and "them." *They* are not the enemy; they are just "us" in another form. Even to confront them is to embrace them, which is to embrace the repugnant aspect of ourselves. To kill them is to love them. The equation of passion and murder is as ancient as our race. To do violence to someone is to desire them. This act is purest among the less conscious species on this world. The lion loves the gazelle so much he devours every edible morsel of its flesh. Only the greatest passion would spring him into action. The laws of nature are such that he cannot love and also preserve. But if you asked the lion (and he could answer), he would preserve the lamb in flesh unto eternity.

Nothing separates the militarist from the warrior as substantially as weapons delivered from the air and the computerized battlefield. The very machines we use to butcher and process our food we have turned against ourselves in ultimate form. There can be no love expressed in the modern war, only a kind of sterile intimation of terror in the absence of either rage or compassion. We are surrounded by a relentless robotized machinery that denies even our existence. Yet the modern war has its karma too, and even without blood on our hands, we are transformed by effects of our collective actions, from the slaughter of the last elephants and whales to the concentration camps of chickens and cattle and the radioactive missile arsenals. We still await the warrior, the knight, in whatever shape he or she may take.

*   *   *

Psychotherapy also involves a process of change between two individuals in a polar relationship. Although convention would have it that only the person seeking therapy is affected, in fact both parties are profoundly altered by the transference that takes place. In traditional Freudian analysis the exchange is entirely verbal, and its goal is to startle the subject into seeing his or her life differ-

ently. Therapy is like a series of brilliant feints or martial maneuvers
that dislodge not the physical body of an adversary but the body
of rigid assumptions that a client adheres to at the expense of his
or her health and freedom. In post-Reichian therapies the therapist
and client actually engage in physical encounters. These may ini-
tially take the form of exercises which are meant to have the same
effect of insight as verbal dialogue, but they may also develop in
the direction of actual physical contact between the parties, including massage, wrestling, and other forms of ritual combat. The
therapist uses every trick possible to bring the somatic effects of
trauma to the surface where they can be contacted.

These therapies have now begun to rediscover methods that
resemble the training of ancient warriors in other cultures. Aikido,
t'ai chi ch'uan, and capoeira have all been used clinically to initiate psychodynamic changes. In this context we might well ask if
a martial training is not always a particular form of healing, and,
likewise, a cure simply a training posed in a psychoanalytic model.
Marine bootcamp and primal-scream therapy approach each other
from radically different models with opposite intents; yet their
experience can be identical. The organism does not ask the intention of the training; it simply responds to what is being done to it.

In general, classical martial artists are more experienced in
terms of physical training and development than either drill ser-
geants or radical therapists. They understand the true battle at
the heart of any one of us. They know our weakest link. And they
know our hidden reservoirs of strength. Dignity and compassion
are strategic concepts to them, not empty words.

A person training martially studies the sources of his or her
own energy, learns to interpret the blocks on that energy, and
develops means of expressing relatively unimpeded power. Through
this process each student comes to terms with his or her own fears,
aggressions, and insights, and translates them into effective action. The actual fight is but a small part of martial training, and
it is also therapeutic, for without self-understanding from confrontation the warrior is ineffective. A strong opponent, just like
a psychoanalyst, forces his or her partners to deeper and deeper
levels of self-awareness and also forces them out of styles of ritual

vanity and self-deceit. I have heard one martial artist refer to an experience as ostensibly nontherapeutic as a street mugging in these terms. He said: "These two guys approached me and they wanted to give me much too much energy. I told them they were overly generous and I didn't need that much energy, but they insisted, so I gave it back to them."

The idea that a fight involves two people sharing energy might be a strange one to those involved in the absolutes of victory and defeat, but it is, of course, the foundation of any transformative practice. Most advanced martial artists eventually come to this understanding. They no longer seek contests, only exchanges with other warriors through which both can grow and learn. With mastery comes the loss of desire for combat. Even the most vicious and blundering of fighters are brought closer to each other in the physical reality of the battle and are compelled to exchange insights and healing in the intimacy of contact. Unfortunately, they give too much energy, much more than either of them can control or use, so the therapy transmits mostly their pathologies. America and the Soviet Union have only the choices now to heal or destroy the world.

*   *   *

The recent movie *The Karate Kid* reflects a new image of the warrior that is gradually entering our cultural unconscious. Certainly Carlos Castaneda's accounts of the shaman Don Juan Matus prepared a whole generation to think of self-development as a battle-exchange with supernatural entities. The spiritual warrior has not supplanted the cowboy or battle-hero in our adversarial folklore, but, in an age of cataclysmic weaponry, these seem provincial and unequipped.

Martial-arts films of recent years have moved some degrees from gratuitous blood-spilling, but they remain almost entirely macho and victory-oriented. *The Karate Kid* goes several steps further; first, because it accepts and personifies the positive values of weakness as well as strength, and second, because it shows that martial matters are self-development somatic issues and, hence, exist everywhere, not just among Ninjas. Even naive teenagers with simple romantic and materialistic goals enact the larger dimension of their battles.

Given his earlier direction of *Rocky*, director John Avildsen was an unlikely candidate for making a film like *The Karate Kid*. Though not as superficially brutal as the Ninja shows of recent years, *Rocky* certainly upheld moral absolutism and redemption through violence. Despite its appealing working-class street myths and triumph of the good-guy underdog, *Rocky* glorifies self-aggrandizing fighting and confuses power and fame for dignity (though it bends over backwards to disguise this ambivalence). It is perhaps Sylvester Stallone's ambivalence we see in the film — his struggle with his own macho fantasies and Hollywood ego. The pomp of the music and camera gives him away. It is no accident that half the people in this country think Sylvester Stallone was a boxer (until he became a "soldier").

Rocky is a film about a fight that didn't have to be fought, and Stallone's "comebacks" merely underscore the impossibility of making the "heavyweight championship" a necessary fight or a fight with any texture or moral depth. Even Mohammed Ali could not do it, and his present physical condition reminds us the battle in the ring is *not* symbolic — that fights develop their true meanings not from propaganda but the reality of the exchange. *The Karate Kid* is about a different sort of fight — a fight that could not be avoided. When the "karate kid," Daniel Larusso (played by Ralph Macchio), complains that his teacher is going to get him killed, Mr. Miyagi, the teacher, (played by Noriyuki Morita), replies: "Get killed anyway." Miyagi regrets violence ("Fighting always last solution to any problem"), but he knows that Daniel will be harassed unless he is ready to fight. He is training him so that ultimately he will not have to fight.

In the documentation of an arduous martial training and the struggle of an underdog to win an impossible bout, *The Karate Kid* is superficially similar to *Rocky*. But *Rocky* ends with an ambitious man showing great courage while punching and receiving punches. In the "karate kid's" closing stance an American teenager discovers the *tao*, the balance in the heart of danger, and teaches his tormentors the truth of love and honor at the heart of the fight.

I heard the best summary of this film before I actually saw it. After attending a preview in New York, the editor of a bestselling book on break-dancing in Harlem called me and described it with great excitement as a confirmation of his book:

> But I see now that break-dancing is only the beginning. There's this whole other martial thing that hasn't been touched yet, not really. This kid, he's from New Jersey, and his mother forces him to move with her to L.A., the Valley, because she's got this new job in rockets and computers and she's tired of snow. He's studied a little karate at the Y back home, but when he gets to California all these incredibly tough guys on motorcycles keep beating him up. Then he falls in love with the cheerleader, the girlfriend of the karate champion. So he's got to learn karate to protect himself, but there's only one teacher around, this crazed Vietnam vet whose main slogan in class is: "Show the enemy no mercy." He's got his students screaming: "Kill, kill, kill!" Of course he's the one who's taught all the other kids. So this kid realizes he's not going to be learning karate there, and he's just about resigned himself to getting beaten up all the time and losing the girl when the master appears. But he's been there all the time. He's the handyman, the gardener. The kid has to make a pact to study karate with him — a real heavy-duty sacred pact. But the first day he comes to study, the master has him wax the cars. The second day he sands the deck. He spends the next two days painting the fence and the whole house. And all the time he thinks he's being used, but he's being trained.

This is a magical film, a film about the initiation of an American teenager, through his fears, bravado, and provincialism, into a world of the old ones. ("You wet behind the ears, Daniel San," shouts Miyagi with a belly-laugh, tilting the boat and dumping his balancing student from the prow into the water. "Wet" because he still believes in the end there will be John Wayne fisticuffs at the high corral.) A rock and roll sound track begins Daniel's initiation, sweeping him through events beyond his control. He is driven across the country to a land of palm trees, taken to the beach by a friend who appears magically to guide him the moment he arrives. The after-dark campfire follows on schecule, opening the ceremony. The girl who will enchant him is already there.

Then the motorcyclists rush in, bust up the party, and begin

Daniel's training. In them we recognize conscious or unconscious references to Kennth Anger's *Scorpio Rising*. I say "unconscious" because these wild astrological figures have been absorbed into dozens of American films, projecting their archetypal identity in the violence they sow. Violence without ritual leads to chaos and brutality, but Anger derived his figures partly from Jean Cocteau, and both men took them as aspects of priests at a dark ceremony going back to Egypt and before.

The Karate Kid is more recently reminiscent of Stephen Spielberg's pop occult films *E. T.* and *Poltergeist*, at least in its depiction of American domestic and street scenes on the threshold of supernatural visitation. But *The Karate Kid* is much subtler, for there are no blatant extraterrestrials or ghosts. Instead, a dormant karate master, disguised for four decades as a handyman, finds his first suitable disciple. Or events conspire to reveal master and disciple to each other.

Spielberg makes his everyday Americans into ciphers, caricatures of TV culture: his women are "space cases," and his men are overaggressive idiots. Avildsen empowers his characters: *The Karate Kid* is precisely a film about empowering ordinary human beings. Daniel's mother is tough and insightful; none of her reactions are overemotional or hysterical for comedic effect. She plays a simple role with so much dignity that she not only alters the film but transcends the Hollywood lineage of buffoonish, ineffective mothers. Daniel's girlfriend is trite only to the degree that anyone that age in that milieu would behave somewhat superficially; without her expression of values in the face of materialism, Miyagi's great lesson would lack resonance.

I find it interesting that the scriptwriter and director never considered it necessary to tell you who or where Daniel's father was. It is a small detail, but most films these days buy cheap sentimentality from broken relationships within families. Many people's lives are ruined just by their acceptance of emotional stereotypes, midlife and other crises. Cultural fads over endow mother-daughter relationships, father-son intimacies, and then divorce. *The Karate Kid* is about having the freedom to become what you are, no matter how family and friends behave. It is spare and basic like *Tender Mercies*. A popular film like *Terms of Endearment* spends essentially the entire movie telling you the equivalent of who Daniel's father is, dramatizing soap-opera issues in a way that the characters are robbed of power and of any humanity. A film about initiation cannot afford gratuitous sentimentality.

As a wise New Age teacher on the American screen, Miyagi follows numerous extraterrestrial intelligences, Comanche war chiefs, Jedi knights, and incarnations of Merlin the magician. When the camera turns to him at the end, he recalls Spielberg's leprechaun-seer Yoda. But at this juncture of our culture I prefer the open hand of karate to the light sword of the Jedi (which, in any case, is lifted from the *chi* of t'ai chi ch'uan and then technologized into a weapon of the high frontier).

There is a lot of Don Juan Matus in Miyagi, so it was appropriate that a comedian was cast in the role. Don Juan and Don Genaro made great sport while jousting with powerful spirit forces; Miyagi shows the zen humor of an Oriental warrior, "Where do all these cars come from?" asks Daniel in exasperation when told to wax them.

"Detroit," answers Miyagi.

When Daniel is beaten terribly by five students of the Vietnam vet, Miyagi says, "Boys have bad attitude." And: "No bad karate students, only bad teachers."

"Great," says Daniel. "All I have to do is go talk to their teacher and straighten him out."

In some ways this film personifies a battle between trained killers hired to carry out superpower strategies and an older lineage of Okinawan warriors — a battle fought by their respective disciples in Southern California. (For all his tough-guy posturing, Stallone as Rambo also stands against the same global military bureaucracy, the ones who tried to lose him in the jungles of Southeast Asia.) In another movie, another era, Daniel would have been with Perry and Joey and the last members of the disintegrated "Wanderers" gang, heading out to Haight-Ashbury on the Jersey Turnpike. The sixties and its Aquarian culture are over, so he ends up in the New Wave/Valley culture war-zone where there are no gods and no clues, either of danger or revelation. It's a nastier version of the fifties: the soul must be discovered all over again. (Not so long ago, the worst we imagined our Government might do was assassinate the President — we were morbidly drawn to the Lee Harvey Oswald mystery for two decades. Now we routinely suspect the CIA of things like dealing in cocaine and heroin, hiring assassins to blow up peasant villages, and sending messenger planes into Soviet airspace to get them shot down.)

Miyagi shares with Don Juan an insight into the magic of modern materialistic culture. He understands the power of Southern California as well as its emptiness. His training of Daniel is subtle and brilliant, for he is able to become his teacher without once trashing his culture or forcing him into an uncomfortable hierarchical relationship. He is even able to bake him a junkfood birthday cake complete with candles. Every step of the way, though, he is deepening his student's experience, placing an appropriate spiritual value on each object and event. Thus the training goes well beyond karate.

It turns out that Miyagi is also a World War II hero; his pregnant wife died in an American internment camp while he was fighting in Germany. During one drunk and sorrowful evening Miyagi reveals this secret, and he and Daniel become compatriots. Daniel discovers the pain and bitterness his teacher had to overcome to regain his balance. This is Miyagi's greatness. He transcends all these potential limitations, including the racial prejudices that would ultimately undermine the friendship. Toward the end of the film he presents Daniel with one of the most pure and heartfelt gifts ever in the American cinema: after the birthday cake, Daniel gets to pick from the cars he waxed, and the keys are already in the one Miyagi knows he will choose. The teacher gives it without binding his disciple to gratitude. It's simply a matter of, "Drive carefully," and mutual delight. Something Daniel's mother never could have afforded is passed down to him by a man they imagined even poorer than they, a man who owes them nothing, to whom they owe everything.

As long as there are dark warriors in the world, there will have to be a fight. One reason *The Karate Kid* carries such mythic power is that it touches on the issue of war and self-defense without trapping us in the battle between pacificism and militarism. We have very few morally acceptable images for violence. The pacificists would generally urge us to turn against the fight, and the militarists give us fights that are excessive, indulgent, and strategically meaningless. *The Karate Kid* is a film about fighting that brings fighting to an end, without rhetoric. It takes a strong step toward pacificism, not by refuting or denying violence but by being a vehicle through which we can experience and transform some of the violence in ourselves.

1984

ABOUT THE BOMB

preface to *Nuclear Strategy and the
Code of the Warrior*

When a new gift, a new possibility, is given to the earth, it is always presented in two ways — in unconscious form, and in conscious form. In the hydrogen bomb we recognize the unconscious form of a power hitherto unknown on earth. We await the demonstration of the same power in conscious form, that is, incarnate in living beings. — Rodney Collin

The atomic bomb is the real Buddha of the West, a perfect detached sovereign apparatus. Unmoving, it rests in its silo, purest actuality and purest potentiality. It is the embodiment of cosmic energies and the human share in these, the highest accomplishment of the human race, and its destroyer; the triumph of technical rationality, and its dissolution into paranoia. Its repose and its irony are endless. It is the same to the bomb how it fulfills its mission, whether in silent waiting or as a cloud of fire. For it, the change of conditioned states does not count.
As with a Buddha, all there is to say is said by its mere existence. It is not a bit more evil than reality, and not a hair more destructive than we are. It is already completely incarnate, while we in comparison are still divided. — Peter Slutterton

Nuclear war sits as a kind of zen riddle in the heart of modern civilization. There is no resolution, no relief, and no way of avoiding the consequences. We find ourselves staring not only at the end of consciousness but the end of history and the end of time. It is almost unbelievable that we could bring this on ourselves and our world; yet we stand at the brink without many ways of turn-

75

ing back. Our own individual deaths, grounded in biological mortality are overwhelming enough, but to have a poisoned silence sweep the Earth moments after our own extinction, to have nothing living follow us, is unendurable. It represents the triumph of the deadliest gods and the demise of nature itself. In the shadow of this unimaginable event we go on day after day, continuing to engage the complexities of our existence. The threat that all this activity could be sheared off, eradicated and scorched into nothing in the space of hours, is the cosmological hallmark of the twentieth century. It is where we have come, out of the various decadent religions of the nineteenth century, into a rising (seemingly irresistible) tide of global materialism (and global nihilism), ruled by the rigorous but rigid forces of pure quantity — a quantity that has now swelled to its inevitable fruition in a bulbous malignant bomb, a bomb that could return all our dissatisfaction and torpor to the cosmic unconscious from which it came. We have become compulsively scientific, image-less — and now an anti-sun has arisen from our very minds. It is naive to think that this is only a political and strategic crisis; it is the physicalization of our crisis of faith, our loss of inner meaning and courage. The warhead is the collective recoil of our spiritual conscience; that is why we cannot wrench free of it or pull back from its compulsion. Only the process of engaging the riddle, of staring unflinchingly through its deadly ruses, is now productive — not as a solution (of course), but as a way of awakening ourselves to who we are and why this is happening to us.

I don't remember when I first became aware of the implications of nuclear weapons, but it was very close to my awakening to the culture itself, probably around third or fourth grade. I no longer remember a time when I did not fear a terrible blinding end. While still in grade school I turned on the radio in reaction to any unexplained and prolonged siren (and by now have done so at least a hundred times in my life, always to be reassured, strangely, by the ongoing inane chatter of America on the dial; ultimately, the chatter is disturbing in another sense, for it maintains the twenty-four-hour-a-day mindlessness and commerciality that beg the crucial questions of our lives — even when they pretend to address them, as in pseudo-serious talk shows). Yet turning on the radio assured me that America was still there.

Nowadays people are more conscious of "the bomb" than they were during the fifties, but that does not make them "bomb"-wiser. Avoiding holocaust is a daily meditation that, like all koans, changes, at the speed of attention. There is no automatic "correct" position.

The longer one lives with the dragon the humbler they become in its teeth. Mindless anti-war activism is another form of bellicosity in the guise of renunciation of violence. Sometimes peace activists are as rigid in their strategies for removing the nuclear threat as any "warmonger." I don't see real compassion for the human condition in this stance. It's more: this is my allegiance, this is what I'm for, and of course I'm on the right side. They want to ram their version of peace and love down everyone's throat. In people shouting peace I sometimes hear only a narcissistic masquerade of denial—pure suppression of their own inner truths. Once, years ago, when I objected to my five-year-old daughter being dragged on peace marches by her alternative school, I got shouted down by parents accusing me either of *supporting* nuclear war or of not understanding the direness of the threat. Yet afterwards in her life, those marches had very subtle, negative consequences.

Nuclear weapons represent far more than stupid generals and unenlightened technicians. People and politicians have fought wars mostly from desperation and necessity, have built weapons in the confusion of mixed conscious and unconscious strategies, often with the goal of ending war. As a species, our ambivalences and nightmares stand out; even when we form implacable antlike armies and carry out atrocities, we are struggling with unconscious demons and on the verge of redemption. One might as well be anti-death or anti-disease as anti-war in the absolute sense. The warriors are inside us, to be embraced and understood, perhaps millennia from now to be ritualized into protectors of all sentient beings. Even the nuclear bomb is inside us, and we must accept the wisdom of its message if we are to avoid its retribution.

Paradoxically, we must also depend on the members of the anti-war movement to raise our consciousness; their outrage and discomfort are an essential breakout of our dormant malignancy—most powerful and curative when they are least rigid: when they bear exotic death's heads and corpse dolls and put on underworld dances; least effective when they are reduced to bumper-stickers, regimented marches, and chanted slogans. These latter activities merely polarize people into ideological camps. Nuclear weapons must awaken us to an event outside politics, even outside consciousness and outside history. They must incite a wild revival of ancient warriors in us.

Rob Brezsny writes:

> We need the bomb because only the tease of the biggest, most original sin can heal us. The bomb is blind, a fake, a trick memory we're sending ourselves from the future that shocks us better than all the Christs and cancers and UFO's. . . . The bomb has been with us since the beginning of time because it's the imagination of the end of time.
>
> We have supernatural powers and genetic potentials so undreamed of that they will feel like magic when they come. But they remain dormant in us until we're scared shitless not just of our individual deaths but also of the extinction of the human archetype. [1]

We must awaken, we must make conscious some of what is unconscious, or we will blunder into Armageddon. The anti-war movement, though relatively powerless in superpower terms, is a faint but crucial beacon for consciousness at this time. Unless superior beings are guiding us or a magus in the soul of the planet is holding back holocaust, we must rely on ourselves to stay awake, even if we must do it dogmatically in an age of dogma. Each day we do not use the bomb is a deepening of our understanding; a practice of restraint.

So the images and symbols of nuclear activists are collectively healing, though in individual cases they may irritate people and alienate closet advocates by their unexamined righteousness. It is too late now to plan an elegant defense. We must make use of what arises spontaneously; we must use existing energy to create new energy, always billowing toward an unknown goal, an unforeseeable resolution. That is what the atom teaches us anyway: pure energy from mass, limitless power from the minute particles of creation. To that we might add the Buddhist precept: that all energy is (in the first place) mind too.

In making images of the end of time and the destruction of living beings and whole cities we startle ourselves, harangue ourselves, and even pity ourselves, but we also often lead ourselves back simply to anger at the nuclear establishment for doing this to us. It is more important to find ways to empower ourselves and to take responsibility, even for acts which are not individually ours. In any case, the so-called "pro-nuclear" position is not that vulnerable. The majority of nuclear-weapons-advocates are equally disheartened by the present impasse and its implications; they argue that destruction may, in the end, be unavoidable and that, in any case, it is not avoidable by a retreat from nuclear weapons. The debate goes back and forth without resolution. The nuclear-advocates argue that the only way to avoid the use of such weapons is to deter war by a balanced arsenal. The corresponding anti-nuclear position is that deterrence is short-term only; if the weapons are built they must ultimately be used, either by error or misjudgement if not by arrogant calculation, and then the whole accumulated stockpile will go off, destroying life on the planet. To this the advocates argue: well, even if that is to be, deterrence is still our only hope because if we do not use the weapons to deter our enemies, they will be used anyway, either on us in our weakness or to blackmail us into surrender; then the world will be conquered by a ruthless dictatorship and there will be decades if not centuries of suffering. A humanist might then question if even that were not better than destruction of life itself; after all, every dictatorship eventually crumbles from within. However, this is not a debate that we can reasonably expect creatures at our level of evolution with our brief lifespans to resolve. No one is worrying about fifty years from now or even twenty years from now. They are trying to get through the next twenty-four hours, then the next month. Nuclear weapons are on the level of interest rates: metaphysical questions can be answered only through living.

Anti-nuclear writings express some of the new level of vigilance that has come since the ascension of Ronald Reagan. It took a gung-ho nuclear-arms-race advocate and an uncompromising militarist to awaken people to the fact that they were already half-awake to a world dangerously overarmed with nuclear bombs. A subtle almost inexpressible change has occurred, and even though it is difficult to trace or spell out, it has given rise to a mass movement. Nuclear vigilance and nuclear terror have been with us since Hiroshima, but people were lulled by the non-bellicose rhetoric of our leaders and the seeming mutual commitment of us and the Russians to detente. The mere fact that we have gone without a world war for a time longer than the time between World War I and World War II is reassuring to people: We have survived both the Cuban Crisis and our fear of an implacable "Red Chinese" foe.

But these reassurances are hollow in light of the actual danger: Ronald Reagan has done a service for nuclear consciousness; he has brought the characters of *Dr. Strangelove* to life and shown that they were not mere fictive exaggerations (though they were alive and among us even before he took office). He has created the living image of a Hollywood president of uncertain emotional depth and wisdom who believes in the *Book of Revelations* as a literal deific prophecy. But he did not invent the dilemma; he is a symptom of our wish to deny the global crisis in all its aspects and blame the Russians. It is a terrible oversimplification to think that one person or even nation could create a problem of this scale. Ronald Reagan is a specter of our somnolent sense of urgency, despite the fact that he may also blunder into the dreaded nuclear war. He has made our situation worse, but he has also ended the latency period of nuclear consciousness, and in that sense he has helped to improve other aspects of the situation. Without him we might not actually *be* more safe; we might only *seem* more safe. *Dr. Strangelove or: How I Learned to Stop Worrying and Love the Bomb* could not have been written today because we no longer feel the same irony or distance from the madness.

Historical political writing of the sort done by Freeman Dyson and Thomas Powers represents a new and earnest public dialogue that is more typical of the 1980s. Both authors present the very ordinary practical difficulties that contribute to an extraordinary crisis. In *Weapons and Hope* Dyson traces and documents the differing views of warfare between ourselves and the Soviets and

shows how we will be unable to negotiate arms reductions as long
as we live in two opposed interpretive frameworks and value systems. The American military accepts nuclear deterrence as a reality
and purports to defend our populace behind its imaginarily concrete shield. The Russians, with their more recent direct experience
of bloody wars and invasions on their own soil, view war as an
uncontrollable and unpredictable pandemonium which, once un-
leashed, can take any wild course. They are not as involved in
the fictive war-games that American planners honor. Of course
neither side maintains an absolute position, but in terms of strategies of defense they worship incompatible gods.

According to Dyson, when the Russians say that they will survive a nuclear war, they are merely stating a centuries-old national credo — not just for war but for their ancient civilization.

They conceive of themselves as the survivors of barbarian
hordes from Asia, Napoleonic armies, and a Nazi war machine.
They are too primitive, even with their mastery of the technology
of the atom, to be bought off by our slick marketing of "deterrence." If *their* weakness is stubborn unexamined ideology, ours
is our susceptibility to mercantile images. They have a rigid bureaucracy; we have a Madison Avenue government. In trying to
sell the Russians deterrence as an assured and fully-tested product (and the mode of arms reduction that goes with it), our government is asking them to buy our definition of reality. They, on the
other hand, continue to offer a reality so harsh and brutal that
we see no safeguard in any compromise or world worth sharing
with them.

As Thomas Powers points out, one of our ploys then is to
bankrupt the Russians by trapping them in an arms race they cannot afford. With a high-frontier star-wars defense we try to im-
pel them into our modern high-credit reality. But in the process
we may bankrupt ourselves and the world as well, bringing on
a different global cataclysm. And, in any case, they will always
steal our secrets (atom bombs, computer chips, satellites, etc.),
whether they actually do or we imagine they do. We are part of the
same superpower conspiracy to control the world by quantity, to
bind the Third World to our image. On the level of espionage and

counter-espionage, there are no longer enough patriotic loyalties
to keep national secrets from either side. Once the international
spy experiences the truth of the global corporate conspiracy, he
is more interested in naming his price and getting his share of the
pie than defending the rhetorical ideals of his homeland. Powers
lists the mirrored atrocities (and accusations of atrocities) of both
sides:

> Q: *What about Poland, Hungary, Czechoslovakia?*
> A: What about Guatemala, Cuba, Chile, Indonesia, Iran?
> Q: *What about Afghanistan?*
> A: What about Vietnam?
> Q: *What about Hafizulla Amin?*
> A: What about Ngo Dinh Diem?
> Q: *What about Masaryk?*
> A: What about Lumumba?
> Q: *What about Sakharov?*
> A: What about Martin Luther King?
> Q: *What about the kulaks?*
> A: What about the Negroes?
> Q: *What about the purges, Gulag, Lubyanka, Siberia?*
> A: What about Dresden, Hamburg, Hiroshima, free-fire zones,
>   Agent Orange?
> Q: *What about the SS-20?*
> A: What about Pershing, GLCMs, SLCMs, ALCMs?
> Q: *What about fifty thousand tanks in Eastern Europe?*
> A: What about the neutron bomb?
> Q: *What about world revolution and the triumph of Com-
>   munism?*
> A: What about "the last best hope of mankind"?
> Q: *What about Khruschev, "We will bury you"?*
> A: What about Sen. Richard Russell, "If we have to start over
>   again from Adam, I want to be sure he's an American"?[2]

"'What do you think spies are,' asks John Le Carré's secret
agent: 'priests, saints and martyrs? They're a squalid procession
of vain fools, traitors too, yes; pansies, sadists and drunkards,
people who play cowboys and Indians to brighten their rotten lives.
Do you think they sit like monks in London, balancing the rights
and wrongs? . . . This is a war. It's graphic and unpleasant because
it's fought on a tiny scale, at close range; fought with a wastage
of innocent life sometimes, I admit. But it's nothing, nothing at

all beside other wars — the last or the next.'"[3]

It would seem that we are left with little choice now: either a grueling daily war or thievery and deceit that robs us of our national resources and identities, or the end of civilization itself. It is no wonder that ideological purists build shelters and await the end of the present civilization and the beginning of the next with anticipation and hope. Of course, the scientific establishment has now decreed a "nuclear winter," which will destroy all life on Earth after the exchange of bombs. Their scenario may be accurate, but it is just another attempt at deterrence, and to the peasant reality of both the Soviets and the Third World it must still look like an American public-relations scheme.

Once again, our self-importance betrays us, betrays even our humanitarian and philanthropic intentions. We must not forget that the majority of people in the world do not have a life that many in the West would be willing or able to lead, and their numbers in Mexico, India, China, Africa, etc., are increasing dramatically. We likewise must not forget, and be willing to look within ourselves to see that our own pious horror at the destruction of the Earth is at least partially linked to the high-percentage share of the Earth that we hold. How much less might be our moral outrage and terror if we each held our appropriate fractional amount of the planet's resources? But then no nation would have the capacity or the need to assemble nuclear arsenals. So self-examination should be part of the raising of our consciousness — on this issue alone if no other. The Third World has always suspected Western liberalism, and that is why poor nations often ignore our messages of peace and seem to support Soviet stands, even against their own self-interest. It is their way of protesting not our monopoly or our greed (as *they* are often just as avid for the same goods); it is their way of protesting our arrogant pieties. They do not begrudge us the sword, but they find laughable the notion that we expect still to control the world's wealth by our superior culture without the sword. Their whole lives have taught them the sorry relationship between power and justice. They don't want apocalypse either, but sometimes they must feel that any disruption of the present order would be an opportunity.

Our own credo of deterrence does have one advantage over the Russians' stubborn decree that they will somehow survive: we recognize, if in the wrong way and for the wrong reasons, that we are in a new world-age and the old rules don't pertain anymore. Ideological rigidities no longer have the same power. But a spiritual transformation is needed, not just a computerized war-game. We intuit, dimly and at a distance, that unrestrained World War must become archaic or played out only hypothetically in symbolic replicas. We do not see that our ideological rigidities, cruelly masked as democracy and freedom, must also be reexamined and transformed in a way that takes into account the present state of sentient life on our planet. One deterrent means nothing without the other; the atomic weapon is just a technological rigidity to support an ideological one. But we have taken the first unconscious step into a new ritual and a new millennium. There *is* a lesson in not yet having fought with nuclear weapons — if only we can grasp its real meaning in time.

Dyson and Powers emphasize a simple but key point: nuclear weapons do not actually increase military capability. They freeze nations into positions of not being able to fight any war, even of self-defense; and they invite nuclear arming by another enemy. They are, in a sense, the demise of the military profession, its replacement by computers and hypothetical wars — with greatly increased danger and risk, at no increase in security. The early atomic scientists also thought of the nuclear bomb as the end to war as we knew it, but unless the military fully accepts this, we can rely only on fortune and rationality to prevent the absurd and tragic use of strategically meaningless weapons.

The notion that nuclear weapons are useless and that the vast sums of money necessary for their manufacture and upkeep could be better spent is probably one of the most workable practical solutions to nuclear war, though the idea of the same money going for different weapons would hardly be attractive to pacifists. If we take the position that war will always be hell and that warring nations will fight with what weapons they have (and we are very far from a peaceful planet), then at least we might hope to buy some time by tailoring our arsenals to fightable wars. As Dyson

shows, we can keep our hi-tech defense and move into new areas
of miniaturized weapons, but we don't have to destroy all life on
the planet. This is his ordinary solution to an extraordinary problem. It represents also Gary Snyder's hope that nuclear weapons
become tabooed, deeply tabooed — in Dyson's sense not because
they are immoral but because they are impractical.

We must face the fact that nuclear weapons are neither the
only epidemic on this planet nor the only peril of our condition. We
are born against all odds onto a pagan, sorrowful world that has
seemingly arisen from conflict, murder, and strife among its living creatures. We are in competition with other life-forms for the
resources of this planet, and we are embattled within our own
species. Nuclear war is a symptom of this dilemma, but it is not
the malignancy itself. Our inability to undo its grip is also our
inability to solve the more fundamental paradox and inequity of
our situation. If we somehow magically eliminated nuclear weapons, some other biological, cosmic, or psychological threat would
replace them as the most advanced symptom — until we reached
the disease itself. Even without the bomb our situation is desperate.

At the turn of the century we thought of war as an interlude
in civilization — a madness, a distortion of ordinary life. But Freud
pointed graphically to what we already suspected: a hidden and
unfathomable unconscious realm from which our hostilities arise —
irrationally and unpredictably, not even as pure instincts but as
the distortions of instincts (archetypes, Jung later said, after the
Nazis — powerful entities we shun and fear at grave risk of being
possessed by them). And Toynbee pointed to a series of cataclysmic
wars that did not seem to be sated by either the first or second
global outbreak. It will take a great deal more than skillful diplo-
macy and good intentions to avoid destroying our civilization.

We exist to a large degree at the mercy of unconscious forces,
and we must bring some crucial aspect of them to expression in
our lifetime. Those forces are ultimate, and real, and bigger than
we are. They are not in a position to show compassion to us; only
we have that power from our human-ness. So we must face them
as they are, face ourselves as we are, not as we would like to be.
The answer to nuclear weapons is not just abnegation of violence,

hatred of hate, destruction of the destroyers; it is a new order of culture, a new ceremony, which will return these gods to a less menacing position.

The metaphysical question posed by nuclear war is like the question of creation itself: will everything really come to an end? Will all life-forms be destroyed, or will some survive and evolve in new directions? Will people survive in small numbers and fight (or not) Einstein's Fourth World War with bows and arrows? If the Earth is destroyed, is this then the destruction of everything? These questions have been asked by other generations for other reasons. We cannot know what spirit realms might succeed this reality, but we must face the spiritual consequences instead of our own science-fiction apocalypse.

Brezsny makes it into a chant:

> Bless the fear. Praise the bomb. Oh God of Good and Evil Light, let the great ugly power fascinate us all now, hypnotize us and fix our terror so precisely that we become one potently concentrated demonic imagination, a single guerrilla meditator casting an irreversible spell to bind the great satan bomb. There will be no nuclear war.[4]

But if we engage in nuclear war and wipe out this world, and there is no other aspect of our creation, then we will have either fulfilled our pathology or given in to the pathological aspect of our nature. There will be a silence like that that preceded us. But even if the spirit worlds go on from here into other realms, and we wipe out this world, we will not enter some heaven or hereafter of the saved, scot-free. We will have to remake this world elsewhere through what is left of our spirit, and it will be all the harder and will take all the longer (in cosmic time), and we will have to do the hard yoga we did not do here. The Christian fundamentalists are simply wrong in expecting they can play Armageddon and then ride happily beside God into the Kingdom of Heaven. Nothing in nature works this way. There was work to do before the bomb, there is work to do to prevent the bomb, and there will be work to do after the bomb, whether we fire it or bury it.

1984

ABORIGINAL ELDER SPEAKS IN OJAI

We scanned the skies with rainbow eyes and saw machines of
    every shape and size.
We talked with tall Venusians passing through.
And Peter tried to climb aboard but the Captain shook his head
And away they soared,
Climbing through the ivory vibrant cloud.
                            —David Bowie

In their own "Dream Time" in the outback of an enormous South
Pacific island the native men and women of Australia seem to be
the keepers of a certain aspect of the human mystery—an aspect
that split off with them when they turned south out of Asia millennia before the written word. By comparison with the civilizations
of both East and West they are like beings from another planet
or dimension. When *East West Journal* asked me if I'd like to write
an article about an Australian shaman's participation in a ceremony of warriors in Ojai, California, I took it as a rare opportunity to experience this ancient and obscure teaching firsthand.

My previous most recent experience with Aboriginal material
came just a year before when Warwick Nieass, a Buddhist painter
and Euro-Australian, visited the San Francisco Bay Area to give
a series of lectures and slide shows on Aboriginal life, and to col-
lect both funds and participants for a camel journey to be led across
the sacred outback by Australian elders. Nieass' talks confirmed
the remaining vitality of native culture, even under wholesale attack by Western bureaucracy and junk food. A cadre of uncor-
rupted natives maintained the initiation rites and spiritual traditions and continued to live off a tremendous diversity of plants

and animals, the culinary use of which was almost totally unknown to Europeans. One of the purposes of the camel trek was to document the ethnobotany and ethnozoology of the desert and add them to the planet's written compendium of resources; another goal was to make a connection between the elders of various Aboriginal tribes and peoples from North and South America, Europe, and Asia. The religion of the Aborigine was finally to be reunited with the other great spiritual traditions of the Earth — in its native setting where it was wed to the sacred power points of the land.

From Nieass' presentation it was clear that psychic visioning, active dreaming, and rigorously trained meditation are all parts of the Australian heritage. Nieass felt that he was a better Buddhist and painter for living in the outback and participating in its life-cycle and mysteries. His tale recalled Carlos Castaneda's encounter with Don Juan Matus, an experience which (whether actual or mythological) has come to stand for the surviving native shaman in the late twentieth century.

To get from Berkeley to Ojai involved driving across the Bay Bridge to catch an early flight from San Francisco to Santa Barbara; then, after an hour's journey above the coast, renting a car, driving south along 101 for about 20 miles; and finally turning east into the mountains and driving 50 miles to the campground. As a displaced Easterner, I have always found West Coast landscapes forboding — their dryness, their uninhabited distances. I recognized here the same topography of power spots I had seen in Wyoming, northern Idaho, and around Mount Shasta: miles of arid land suddenly exploding in a great lake. The outpouring of birds and flora in a desert context is itself a shamanic event.

Then my map led away from the water, and by the time I reached the campground mountain the plastic inside the car was a steam-bath, even with the windows open. I was quite late, so I parked at the end of the row and stepped out into the sagebrush air; a lizard skittered through the dust onto a rock and stopped there. Lightheaded, I yawned and adjusted. I felt as though I had been travelling a week, and it was barely past noon. An open tent stood at the top of the hill, its soft fabric luminescent. I slipped in quietly and took a chair in the back. Guboo Ted Thomas sat on a small dais, a white-bearded elder dressed modestly with a star-inside-a-star medallion of beads around his neck, native instruments beside him.

Guboo (literally "good friend") was in the middle of a story about the emu and the frog. That story led to another, and then another; he would interrupt each with songs, political and spiritual asides, and descriptions of the Australian landscape. Given the dramatic literature advertising this show I had expected participatory reenactments of some of the great Aboriginal animal rituals. This was, after all, a millennial occasion—the bringing of the Dream Time to North America, the exchanging of sacred shields. I gradually had to reattune myself to the more modest event at hand. It was actually a lecture, and Guboo spoke perfect, almost ministerial English, his accent putting an occasional charming "h" before vowels ("Mother h'Earth," "h'animals").

Guboo said the Dreaming allowed him to look back in the past and to go with his mind into the future. "You can't turn the wheel back," he said. "But what the white man has done to my people the Great Spirit is now changing. I see a great white wave leaving Australia, sweeping Europe, America too." It was a wave representing the spirit of his people, the Yuin Tribe. "We can link up. We can change Reagan's mind. We can change Bob Hawke's mind in Australia. We can do that by coming together in love."

Throughout his talk, Guboo made it clear that the elders had chosen him to bring a message to the rest of the world. "I don't work in my own strength," he said. "It's the Great Spirit that leads me. When he says go, I go." But insofar as he was willing to state it explicitly Guboo's message was so simple and straightforward as almost not to bear saying. "We've lost respect for Mother h'Earth today. You know, they clear it and call this progress. They don't know what danger they're doing. I believe we're in the last days of the chapter of the Bible, *Revelations,* unless we come together in love. The Great Spirit now tells me I should go and talk to the people, and that's why I'm here today. It's not the color of people's skin that's important. Inside the body is the soul, most precious. So it is wonderful to be here and talk to you. I've looked at the past; I've seen the future. The Dreaming is something else. I used to hate the white man, but the Great Spirit, he gave me a heart as big as a cabbage."

Aside from its Christian apocalyptic moral, Guboo's message was benign enough as stated, but I found myself wondering why a person of his ostensible level of training would travel such a long distance to deliver it. After all, most people are aware that we'd be better off living in peace with each other and in harmony with nature. The great question is: How? To answer that we need a medicine teacher, a shaman from the Dreamtime like one who has not yet been seen. But Guboo's opening comments more resembled a provincial hippie interpretation of native thought than an authentic Australian teaching. At the same time, I wasn't sure that Guboo wasn't equally aware of the triteness of what he was saying and his numbing effect (he spoke in curious non-sequiturs). At moments I felt he was teasing us, throwing up a mirror to our clichés of who he might be. I still don't know.

On matters of The Dreaming Guboo was far more eloquent, though he did not treat it esoterically; he described only its exterior artifacts and effects. Most significantly he made clear that The Dreaming is not just a passive myth-account of the creation of things and the journeys of the ancestors (as early anthropologists reported); it is a living telepathic experience, a meditation with a long training focusing a tremendous power.

"We have no phones to ring people up, no wireless. We do it with our minds. We send messages from mountain to mountain, to mountain, thousands of miles away. We know exactly what they mean. That's how we keep in touch with our people." In short, he was acknowledging psychic power as a collective cultural experience; and, although the audience took it at face value (probably because they were there to believe such things), I found it a shocking claim with monumental implications. Paranormal episodes have been reported and even well documented by parapsychologists for decades, but Guboo was saying that this was an ordinary everyday ability of the Aborigine and was used as mundanely as a telephone. "From the power points of Australia we can tune into America, tune into h'England."

After his talk I sat by the side of the tent and asked him if he could communicate telepathically from here with people in Australia.

"Yes, that's right, I can. I can sit down and do my meditations, and I can tune into other countries, all over the world. The Aboriginal people have done it 40,000 years or more."

The Dreaming is, in fact, tantamount to telepathy. It is precisely by one's entering into an experience of The Dream Time that telepathic communication becomes possible; only then is one transported outside of space and time. In such a trance the Dreamer can see the land as it was at creation, the ancestors as they came, the animals in spirit form, the beginnings of all things. It is one vision, one meditation, and even includes ordinary night dreaming.

Guboo described how his grandfather was sitting on a rock with the tribal elders when "the great white ghost ship of Captain Cook suddenly appeared off the coast. My grandfather said: 'This is the end of civilization,' And it was the end of civilization. The white man brought us every kind of poison, every kind of disease." From the Aboriginal viewpoint, the Europeans did not so much bring power to an impoverished land as they diminished power in a great spiritual civilization. But since the Aborigine had always foreseen the White Man in The Dreaming, he knew who was coming.

With marvelous detail Guboo described another aspect of The Dreaming, a practice much more extensive and far-reaching than the geomancy it is usually assigned to: Nature spirits are hidden in the rocks and trees and make themselves visible when a spiritual person is present. "I wasn't born in a house," Guboo almost chided us. "I was born in the bush. I'm part of the environment. I touch a tree, I feel its love. In the morning, when I go out to the mountain and do my ceremonial, the birds, the h'animals, they all stop, they listen to me till I finish the ceremony; then the birds start singing again."

Alfredo Quarto, Guboo's biographer, stood up and gave testimony to the shaman's amazing power; he was followed by a woman who had spent time with Guboo in the bush. They said that animals just appeared in his presence, that birds came right up to him and started singing, and that enormous numbers of spirits manifested in rocks and trees around him. The rocks themselves suddenly took on faces and emitted palpable energy. Quarto recalled looking out over the ocean in moonlight and recognizing an intelligent face in the rock staring alongside him. He was hoping that Guboo's visit to America would wake up rocks and trees everywhere from centuries of slumber. He was anticipating the advent of The Dream Time in our country.

Guboo related one occasion when he was standing in the heart of Sydney at an interview; he suddenly asked the photographer to "shoot" because he sensed something there. Then he showed us all the picture. There *was* an enormous face gazing intently out from the rocks just behind him.

Guboo emphasized that these faces are not coincidental patterns, they are the actual spirit beings innervating ancient stone. Areas in which these rock spirits are either perennially active or permanently visible are of course the Aboriginal sacred sites. When Guboo explained how he had gone through great trouble to keep the Japanese paper companies and Australian oil firms from destroying many of the habitats of these spirits, I was reminded of Nieass' slides of the oil-exploration armadas crossing oases of the outback on tractor treads, looking like something from *The Empire Strikes Back.*

"We have no statues of angels to make things sacred," Guboo said. "No cathedrals, no stained glass windows. What we have is much more sacred. We have the nature spirits themselves. These are more spiritual than the man-made church. God put that there, Mother Nature, for the Aboriginal people to sit around and do their meditation!"

He also confirmed the existence of certain global mystery creatures and included them in the geomancy of The Dream Time. The bigfoot, or yeti, known in Australia as the yowee, is one of the nature spirits. The reason no bones or remains are ever found (despite the sightings) is that yowees do not live in the same dimension as we do. They are mischievous spirits, and dance in and out of our plane leaving an acrid odor each time: "The yowee is a very very spiritual animal; he's a part of the Aboriginal ceremonial, and we always communicate with him."

He identified the Loch Ness Monster as another creature of The Dream Time, known in Australia as the Rainbow Serpent. He also pointed out that the links of telepathic communication between mountains are strongest where cosmic paths run between the peaks. "We tune in along the ley lines," Guboo explained. "A most wonderful thing, the mind. The ancestors wandered around in the bush, and they observed and listened, and they learned. Now we can listen to birds, animals, breezes. I can read your mind right now," he told the audience with a sweep of his arm. "I know why you came here. I know who you are."

As a graduate student in anthropology during the late 1960s I discovered that A. P. Elkin was considered the best popularizing ethnographer of the native Australians, but his main book, *The Australian Aborigines*, gave little insight into spiritual matters, organized as it was by traditional academic categories. Elkin characterized the uniqueness of Aboriginal life mainly in terms of the complex system of intermarriage among clans. In the background of this esoteric social life he found extraordinary initiation ceremonies involving genital mutilation, long and painful trainings of medicine men, life-and-death bouts of witchcraft, and an ancient tradition of rock art, cave paintings, boomerangs, and digging sticks. As in so many anthropology books, the author dissected the surface appearance of a people—their customs and bare subsistence—without any sense of the special reality—the phenomenology—of their lives.

Just a little out of this mainstream one can find writings suggesting greater profundity and a deeper psychospiritual existence. In his quest for the roots of "totems and taboos" the Freudian psychologist Géza Róheim collected hundreds of Aborigine dreams. These show a powerful internalizing process. For instance: "I dreamed of a woman who had only one foot, one arm, and one breast. She came from the west and sat near me. Then we flew together into the sky where there was a second earth. We killed two caterpillars and sucked the marrow from their bones. . . . The she-devil led me and I followed her. We came to a devil's camping-place where many bones were lying about; the devils had eaten the souls. . . . They took hold of me and threw me into the fire. New bones, and hot stones, were put into my head and body. Then we came to the home of the one-legged people. They took me to a great hole and said: 'Look inside.' The hole was full of testicles which had been cut off. They gave me one, saying that it was mine. Then I went with the one-legged people and we came to the frogs." [1]

But Róheim interpreted these dreams and the attendant sha-manic rituals according to the strictest Freudian regimens, so in the initiations of medicine men he saw the primal scene of the parents (their copulation in myths of the Milky Way); in sorcerer flying dreams he found erections; and in complex ceremonies of partial castration: compulsion-anxieties of full castration. Once again a Western observer, right at the portal of the mystery, turned back into the biases and pseudo-objectivities of his own culture.

But other Western writers have gone further. In a number of his books the spiritual historian Mircea Eliade has described the creation of sacred time through The Dreaming. The Australian anthropologist W. E. H. Stanner published a series of articles about The Dream Time in various journals during the 1950s. Like Eliade he pointed in the right direction — inward, beyond what he himself knew: "Although The Dreaming conjures up the notion of a sacred, heroic time of the indefinitely remote past, such a time is also, in a sense, still part of the present. One cannot 'fix' The Dream-ing *in* time: it was, and is, everywhen. . . . Clearly, The Dream-ing is many things in one. Among them, a kind of narrative of things that once happened; a kind of charter of things that still happen; and a kind of *logos* or principle of order transcending everything significant for aboriginal man. If I am correct in say-ing so, it is much more complex philosophically than we have so far realised." [2]

The Dreaming transcends ordinary time and space and in-corporates the creation of plants, animals, stones, and stars at the beginning of the universe. An Aborigine passing into The Dream Time might experience days, months, or even thousands of centuries in a passage of seconds.

In more recent years some of the beauty and power of the Aboriginal ceremonies has even been translated onto film. *Emu Ritual at Ruguri* is a straightforward documentation of a several-day-long Aboriginal ceremony. Although one cannot perceive the "inside" of the ceremony, one *can* sense the intensity and duration of attention in the participants—throughout not only the dancing and chanting but the long and seemingly tedious preparation of artifacts. We are watching simple people in deep, sensual states of devotion and performance. No mere exotic symbols hold them to something as subtle as a ritual; it is a primal emotional experience, most apparent at the climax as the weeping initiates are led blindfolded through sacred caves where their elder teachers guide their fingers along the ancient markings in the stone.

Recently these images have been popularized and even politicized in a new Australian cinema. The power of The Dream Time is made explicit in *The Last Wave,* a movie in which charismatic Aboriginal actors (Gulpilil and Nandjiwarra Amagula) bring their voodoo and interior visioning to the cities; at the finale, urban Australia is destroyed by a great ocean wave.

Here The Dreaming is portrayed not as a mere animist myth but a source of physical energy, from beyond the known forces of science, with the capacity to act geologically and meteorologically and to return the land to its aboriginal state. This sort of cosmology has global and apocalyptic implications and is quite a few degrees removed from the extended families of Elkin's quaint blackfellows of the bush. Philip Kaufman pays almost after-the-fact homage to this legacy in *The Right Stuff* by placing the telekinetic fire-transporting ability of the Aborigines on a par with the American space program. John Glenn in his orbital capsule is surrounded by dancing sparks launched from the Australian desert. He has travelled by rocket back into The Dream Time, and, in the absence of his heat shield, is protected blindly by Aboriginal shamans sitting before their fires.

In the Western spiritual mythology of the 1980s the Australians (like the Hopis) are not only "dreaming" their own golden legend-time; they are dreaming all of nature. They are maintaining the sacred hearths for all of us. Cut off from the rest of the species for anywhere from 10,000 to 100,000 years, they have perhaps developed unique parapsychological (and paraphysical) abilities. Their Dream Time is a universal human experience that has become totally unconscious and vestigial in the rest of humanity.

The overall day's events at Ojai, although they brought me closer to a perception of The Dream Time, had a definite dark side, and I left with an uncomfortable feeling. Since I was treated graciously and generously by everyone there, and because I believe in the good work of the Ojai Foundation, I will try to be fair in my assessment. The questions I raise seem to me the hard questions that must be raised in this context. I think they are the questions all of us are asking at one level or another, and they represent the desire and, in fact, the necessity to move beyond staged events to an actual interchange of cultures and spiritual traditions.

Guboo was a speaker at a conference that ran from April 29th to June 3rd and entitled: "Awaken The Dream: The Way of the Warrior," also subtitled: "Ancient Tradition and New Thought from Six Continents." The speakers included Harley Swiftdeer, a native American medicine chief; Lama Chakdud Tulku Rinpoche, a Tibetan lama and doctor; Al Huang, a t'ai chi master and musician; Don José Matsuwa, a 105-year-old Huichol shaman from Mexico; Elie Hien, an African medical doctor, shaman, and herbalist from the Upper Volta; and numerous psychologists and scientists (Rupert Sheldrake, John Lilly, and R. D. Laing, among others). During the long, hot afternoon Guboo shared the podium with Swiftdeer, Hien (and his translator from French), Joan Halifax (the Director of Ojai Foundation), and Gigi Coyle, a woman involved with both dolphin communication and the Australian Dreaming.

I met Joan Halifax soon after I arrived, and I talked to her at some length during the lunch break. She gave me a brief history of the Ojai Foundation: It was built on land with a long spiritual history; once owned by Dr. Annie Besant and the World Theosophical Association, the "spiritual foundation" was called Human

Dimensions West and was in some financial trouble and direc-
tionless when Halifax took over in 1979. Professionally, she had
been an anthropologist and had become an expert on global shamanic traditions, studying in the Caribbean, Africa, and the Middle East. She had also swum with dolphins, participated in many
religious ceremonies (as well as LSD experiments), and had been
advisor to the film *Altered States.* When she was working with
Joseph Campbell in New York a medium told her that she would
be offered work on May 21, 1979. This prophecy was fulfilled by
the Ojai offer, and she accepted it despite her lawyer's advice to
the contrary.

When she spoke to me, Halifax was experiencing a tremendous high from the conference. She presented herself as a former
academic now caught in a web of prophecy, initiation, and millennium. She had been chosen. Ojai had been chosen. The "Warrior" conference represented the fulfillment of a 5000-year-old
prophecy: the spiritual leaders from the world's traditions would
come together and share their wisdom and exchange their ritual
shields.

I wanted to believe that this was happening, and if I had been
ten years younger, I probably could have convinced myself that
I was present at a millennial event. However, I have been to too
many events over the years that have advertised themselves as
cosmic turning points, and I have lost some of both my passion
for and terror of millenarianism. I have met shamans, travellers
to other worlds on UFOs, and apocalyptic prophets from various
traditions. Yet none of the people or events lived up to claims and
advance notices; David Bowie's *Memory of a Free Festival* now
seems a fair epitaph for a whole era (to which all of our attempts
to force history into myth are a throwback).

The most extraordinary moments for me have come with
much lower profiles. I wouldn't say that they have come when
I least expected them, but they have come when I thought I was
doing something simple and personal. I have had marvellous visions and intuitions of timelessness and boundless love, and these
have been in an out-of-the-way sweat lodge in northern Idaho;
a t'ai chi class in Berkeley; a Lomi breathing session in Marin.

But the day at Ojai reminded me mostly of the conferences I was forced to attend during my days as a graduate student in anthropology. Only this time the authority was not, by name, academic, it was spiritual — but it was still academic authority, and it mostly lectured me and told me *about* things into which (I was also told) I was not ready to be initiated. I heard Halifax tell the assembled group that "some of us will dance in the mountains, and others of you, who cannot come into the mountains, will dance in the valley." It was meant to suggest stages of spiritual development, but it sounded like power positions in a bureaucracy and academic credentials. It was Joan Halifax, Ph.D.; Harley Swiftdeer, Ph.D.; Elie Hien, Ph.D. I had no problem with that. But all of them spoke of degrees of initiation and of superiority that I found out of harmony with the traditions involved and more in keeping with academic hierarchicalism advertised.

Elie Hien asked if we had heard of the famous Dogon shamans; then he said: "We roll along at 190 kilometers an hour. We go so fast they don't even see our dust." It was a facile line, and my sense was that it was cultivated for audiences at spiritual conferences. It got a huge burst of applause and laughter. He also drew a big response with his rote put-down of science: "The Earth is water, we live in water; the scientists are going to have to discover this someday." They haven't?

Throughout the afternoon I had a sense of violation, though it was very subtle, and I was not always sure what was intentional, what was unconscious, and what I simply misinterpreted. At times I was torn between accepting the authenticity of the visions and being outraged at the relentless marketing of each person's successive spiritual experience. Sometimes I felt the lightness and energy of the spiritual valley, but more often I felt pushed along by the schedule of activities and the "adult day camp" atmosphere. One problem in Ojai that day was the food. Len Jacobs of *East West Journal* first pointed out (in his review of my book *Planet Medicine*) that I tend to overlook diet in my focus on transcendent myths and symbols. Before he and others raised my consciousness on that issue, I accepted the "feed 'em junk and get 'em back to the conference" attitude of many seminars. The message may be the important thing, but the food is part of the consciousness and overall world view of the organizers. It is never neutral; it always represents a commitment to something. I'm sure Ojai has had more holistic menus, but on Guboo's day participants were offered either turkey or cheese doused in mayonnaise on white bread in cellophane and a can of Dr. Pepper or Lipton's tea.

Then Harley Swiftdeer, who was not an Indian and smoked cigarettes during his presentation (neither of which of course negated his message), tried far too hard to push all the traditions into one hat. He started out thanking "Joan and the rest of my brothers and sisters here on the panel." He went on to talk about "living only to die, dying every moment you live. . . . We can go from this reality into any other reality. . . . We can collectively dream with the plant and animal kingdoms and human memory. . . . We can harmonize, resonate with all things—Grandmother Earth, Grandfather Sun, Sister Moon. . . . Elie, myself, and the dolphins activate the waking dream so that we are dancing it awake. I'm sure Guboo dreams this way too."

I felt he bullied Guboo into agreeing with this by his forceful and jaunty dominance. He was saying: "Here's the scoop on Dreaming. I'm going to package it for you, put it into categories, and make it possible for you to do it too." But it was a lot of talk, and it was very hot in the tent.

Swiftdeer closed by exhorting the audience to "dream with us—the sacred teachers of the light—dream with the dolphins, swim with the dolphins, make music with the dolphins." Hadn't I once longed to hear just these things said—to believe in an Indian who could speak for Aborigines and dolphins both? But I found only the cynical part of me responding and scoffing. How had I become a traitor to my own cause?

Perhaps Swiftdeer even approached the implied ambivalence of his own message when he wondered, almost offhandedly, "Did I dream the dolphin into my world, or did the dolphin dream me into his world?" This man was either an authentic shaman trying to mainline extremely profound teachings or a mere performer feigning profundity by addressing us like children. Why couldn't I tell the difference?

Halifax opened by declaring the "shape-shifting of a myth of the future, which is also a very ancient myth of the past, of our origins within the great oceans of timeless time." She then described her experience of being "trained" by two friendly dolphins in a tank, culminating in an episode of being swum about, each with a wrist of hers in its mouth: "me and the dolphins in one transcendent moment, transcending culture and nature." When she tried to stay in the tank too long, one of them butted her, gently perhaps for dolphins; it was a bruising slap and awoke her instantly to the greed that had her lingering for extra spiritual goodies when the experience was already complete.

But are dolphins in captivity really capable of being such gurus for us?

Coyle stated her agenda as a "collective consciousness of teachers from many traditions coming together into the same practice, the single Dream Time." On stage she was a curious mixture of tough, hard-won wisdom and New Age jet-setting, self-conscious in a way none of the other speakers were. For instance, she made a point of distinguishing between what she actually knew and her mythic projections. Yet the generic avatar-role afflicted her, as though she were playing a persona of Janis Joplin, Ram Dass, and Debra Winger. Typically — after carefully introducing techniques of dream yoga for "shape-shifting within dream-form" — she said, "but I'm not permitted to give them to you."

In trying to figure out what Guboo really meant to be telling us (or even who he was) I am also trapped in contradictions. He presented multiple faces, and I do not know if they were the multiple faces of the guru-actor or the true medicine man. I do not mean to be ironical; I simply couldn't tell.

After the day's events, when I spoke to Guboo in private, I tried to ascertain if he had really gone along with all that was said in his behalf, especially by Swiftdeer. Swiftdeer's vision was, in itself, moving, but I wondered if an Australian would feel comfortable with it. "I was not sure if you agreed with what was being said this afternoon or were just being polite."

He was silent for a moment, then said: "My talk is bringing

people together in love. There's a lot of people that talk, so I just shut off. There are so many different organizations that are not the right thing. I can always tell when something's wrong, so I just stop at that. No matter what they say or what their belief is, I just go along with them. But I have my own versions of it."

Because of the indirect way in which Guboo speaks, I have no conviction that he was actually referring to the events of that afternoon. He himself told a strange story in the tent: There was a lady in America who had been seeing him for eighteen months in a vision. Then one day he was at the Transformation Center in Sydney, and apparently she knew the man in her vision was going to be there, so she came with her husband. Earlier that day Guboo had told his wife that he was going to get a new car, and when the woman approached him she broke down crying and asked what he wanted. "A land cruiser," he said. "She gave it to me. $15,000 worth. That's what I'm talking about, The Dreaming." It was an almost perfect replica of Ram Dass' story of giving his friend's Land Rover to his guru.

What was missing from Guboo was any sense of mystery and wonder or spiritual transformation. He put forth Australian politics, Dream Time fragments, Christian prophecy, and blunt editorials in series of loosely connected sentences as though every statement were a separate proverb. He seemed most comfortable with quasi-scientific and historical language about the Aborigine: "We're the oldest people on Earth. We go back 40,000 years. We go back before Christ. Anthropologists say we came during the Ice Age. I don't believe that. I believe Aboriginal people were always in place."

Guboo mentioned those 40,000 years at least two dozen times in his hour-long presentation: "We try to show people sacred sites, because we have this oral history 40,000 years now. The anthropologists and archaeologists don't understand what I'm talking about. They think it's crap."

But why was he even showing them?

At another point he said, "The Aboriginal people have listened to the h'animals for 40,000 years. The Dream Time comes easy for Aboriginal people."

"40,000 years" is a European reference point and should hardly be a focus for a *bona fide* shaman. Even the terms "oral history" and "telepathy" come from outside the ceremony; yet Guboo used both repeatedly. He also talked about "erosion, going down all the time, killing marine life." The sentiment was native, but the terminology was Sierra Club.

The audience wanted to like Guboo and wanted him to know they liked him. They were primed with their best Third World demeanor, which unfortunately had the give-away ring of cultural guilt. The questions were polite and respectful. The first person asked, "Does the snake have any special symbolic significance among your people? I know it does among certain Native American tribes."

Hardly the way to get to the bottom of things. It might have been a folklore seminar. Guboo responded in kind: "The rainbow serpent comes up out of the water like the Loch Ness Monster. We see the ripples in the water. So it means a lot to the Aboriginal peoples."

A woman asked, "Are your people still hunters and gatherers?" Anthro./101.

"No, we live in houses like White people. I think the Aboriginal people deserve it."

Did he believe this? Was it the real answer?

To another question about the global impact of the Dreaming he had a surprisingly secular Chamber of Commerce response — how the message of the Yuin was travelling by bicycle across Europe and Japan to Russia, bringing peace and love. "People all over the world can't get over the warmness of the Aboriginal people." Bicycle? Can't get over?

Someone asked him to say a few words in his native tongue. He did. Someone asked him if there were Aboriginal people that had never been touched by the White Man and what kind of life do they live?

"They just roam around — normal." This provoked spontaneous applause, whistles, and one very loud whoop. Someone yelled, "Score, score!"; and someone else said, "All right!" It was as though with that single sentence Guboo had reduced the Western establishment to ashes.

At the end of the proceedings, when Guboo and Quarto were gathering up the instruments and artifacts they had brought, I watched them while realizing that I could not tell whether I was viewing a clever hustler masquerading as an Aborigine elder or a brilliant medicine man travelling in an impenetrable disguise. "This one's ours," he said. "That one's theirs. This, I don't know what this is. Take this one. No, leave that, that's not ours." Was this the circus packing up and moving on?

I have heard too many stories about the wasted Third and Fourth World to believe any more that we can just summon elders to conferences because we are Americans and can pay their plane fares. Our grants and New Age promotions cannot restore shamanism or bring the legitimate representatives of shamanic traditions. And even if they did, these teachers would not reveal their real knowledge to the kinds of spiritual materialists they would run into here.

I emphasize: the goals of the conference were admirable, and the stories told were moving and suggested the direction in which we must go. I just didn't find that the participants could separate mythological desires and fantasies from true events, or, if they could, that they could make their experience of the separation believable to me. The Dolphin Dreaming, which dominated much of the afternoon, was a real case in point. Almost all the speakers, but most notably Swiftdeer, Coyle, and Halifax, discussed trans-species communication with dolphins. They indicated that the dolphins had a tribalism not unlike the Aborigines and shared a Dreaming in which we humans had an important role. Swiftdeer said that the dolphins were "far superior to humans; they've been around much longer, have much larger brains; the sensory input they can handle far exceeds what we can handle." Coyle and Halifax indicated that they had been personally chosen by the dolphins for initiation into *their* Dream Time and that this initiation is part of the gathering of shamans in Ojai and the exchange of wisdom and shields.

The attempt to communicate with other species and the bringing together of the world's shamanic traditions (including the

shamans of other species) are truly significant millennial under-
takings, and I have great respect for the attempt, even the failed
attempt, to accomplish them. If these were truly done, especially
in the present context of world politics and nuclear weapons, our
terrifying science-fiction story would be changed totally in five
years. But in order to continue our individual work, we must be
able to distinguish between the attempt and the actuality; the
speakers at Ojai were not empowering of their audience, and that
was their problem; they tried to claim power. If they had accomplished what they claimed, or even if they had merely attempted
it, they should not have been boasting or strutting as they were.

Perhaps the underlying difficulty with the event was the
assumption that the Australian Dream Time is an equivalent mode
of experience not only to lucid dreaming in the West, but to Buddhist meditation, trans-species communication, and vision-quests
among other native peoples. The goal of the conference was to
bring these forms into an active concordance. But what if they
are not commensurate practices; what if their values lie in their
exclusivity and regionality?

By having Guboo speak and then interact with a "shamanic"
panel, the organizers were betraying their own universalist presumptions. Guboo was notably quiet during the discussion; it is
possible this was because he did not buy the ease with which the
other participants were "exchanging shields" (though there also
was nothing about his performance otherwise that suggested cultural purism or esoteric knowledge. In fact, he reminded me most
of an oldtime ball-player accepting his induction into the Hall of
Fame — in this case, the American Shaman Hall of Fame at Ojai).
Maybe he happily exchanged shields out of public view. But then
none of us saw that Event.

What I was left with finally was the grandiosity of the panelists, their talking down. They didn't realize they were talking
down, but their sense of spiritual self-importance and the epochal
implications of the gathering did away with the usual cautions
and restraints. They could only rehearse what the audience paid
for; and since no one was actually being trained or initiated, the
best they could do was a sort of theatre for which they imported

an Australian to play an Aborigine, an anthropologist to play a shaman, a cowboy to play an Indian, a black shaman speaking Cocteauean French, his translator, etc.; roles that evoked somber epistemologizing and cosmic declarations — the diametric opposite of *Waiting for Godot*, except that that's exactly what they were doing. Any real spiritual depth was masked by spiritual super-starring.

Changes in planetary consciousness suggest big concepts, and we in the West have the luxury to think them. Most people on the Earth merely survive. Yet I think it's out there in the mere and inarticulate survival that the real change will come. In California (and elsewhere too in the West for that matter) people are overly anxious to possess something that has been labelled and marketed as "The New Age." The New Age has become a product: a product of very capitalistic businesses that have mastered anti-capitalist and anti-materialist rhetoric. The marketing of changes in consciousness has more to do with the minority who control the wealth of the world and less to do with the sheer majority of creatures on the Planet. I do believe something big is happening in the West, but I don't claim to know what it is. Just because we have the balance of payments, the factories, the college educations, and the press doesn't mean we have the right to speak for the planet as a whole or the shamanic traditions of the jungle or outback. As Guboo himself said: "You white people have got the gift of gab. But it's not from the heart. So you skip steps. When you skip steps you have to go back and do them over. But you talk yourselves into thinking you're there."

1984

EASY DEATH

a review of *Easy Death* by
Da Free John

Since I began reading spiritual literature some twenty years ago at the age of nineteen, no book has changed my view of the universe more profoundly. Without introducing any symbols of transformation, occult worlds, or spirit beings, Da Free John has spoken directly to the heart of our human situation — the shocking reality of our brief and unbidden lives. Through his words I have experienced a glimmering of eternal life and view my own existence as timeless and spaceless in a way that I never did before. It is as though after all these years of troubled and uncertain mysticism someone suddenly convinced me of life after death. Of course, no one book can have such an effect (and certainly not in a lasting manner), but in *Easy Death* Da Free John has subtly altered my perception by a degree. I still wage a battle of nihilism and transcendence, but it has shifted from a mere divergence of metaphysical scenarios into a lasting riddle at the heart of my nature. The change is small but devastating. Da Free John does not expound theological beliefs or recount true-life tales of return-from-the-dead and reincarnation, he simply demonstrates that ordinary experience is already eternal. His brutal honesty makes it stick.

I should emphasize that I have never met Da Free John nor been to his community or any of his centers. I know his teaching ex-

clusively through the printed word. I began reading him several
years ago because I was curious to know why his were the only
Eastern books in an orthodox Reichian library of anatomy, psycho-
physiology, and bodywork. Their curious titles and bright cartoon-
like covers attracted me. I can remember wondering who this
strange teacher was who had taken on the name of Bubba Free
John (and then later Da Free John). I realize now that many people still wonder this and that the odd name keeps them from the
work. A number of potentially interested readers have spurned
these books on the false presumption that the name was an intentional parody of the role of the guru or the clowning of a self-conscious guru. There is in fact humor in Da Free John's self-charac-
terization, but his names have been chosen for sound spiritual and
etymological reasons. Because of the misunderstanding they have
caused, I think it is important to point out that the work of this
teacher is absolutely serious, simultaneously wise and humble, and
compassionate to the deepest degree. I experience some of the same
lucidity in the printed talks of Chögyam Trungpa and quoted
statements from G. I. Gurdjieff and Don Juan Matus; but, although I don't mean to set Da Free John above other avatars in
any false hierarchy, I find that he speaks candidly on spiritual issues
even these remarkable teachers mythologize or hedge on. It is
because his understanding of his own ignorance is so profound and
incisive as to be chilling.

Easy Death is one of many published collections of the talks
of Da Free John. Together they make up a teaching. I have chosen
this one as representative of the work because it violates very basic
taboos and is a clear statement of our relation to the cosmos and
to eternity.

For the most part the talks in the early part of the book char-
acterize death as we conventionally view it—a magnificent but
horrifying mystery. Da Free John refuses to lure the reader with
promises of heaven or ego continuation: "There is no way to have
any fixed certainty about whether or how you survive your death."
But the mystery of death is no different from the mystery of life
or the mystery of the universe itself. It is impossible to have any
real knowledge about *anything* in the universe. No one has ever

had it or will ever have it: "Not Jesus, not Moses, not Mohammed, not Gautama, not Krishna, not Tukaram, not Da Free John." Even beings on other planets and in other universes and dimensions, no matter how enlightened or how advanced scientifically, can know nothing about reality. Science will merely exhaust us with its discoveries of interminable vastness. Even if our civilization survives for billions more years, our knowledge will not increase in this regard. "Out of nowhere, we are existing in these bodily forms. Look at all of us sitting around in this room here, completely unable to account for anything! Our situation is weird!"

We come into being because the world "represents at least an aspect of our tendency toward experience." But we live under the shadow of death; we cannot evade it; we cannot minimize it. Science, politics, and the modern media all try to propagandize us into seeking absolute fulfillment on this plane, but any happiness achieved on that basis will be superficial and transient. We exist in preparation for an extraordinary experience that everyone has undergone, even the ordinary aunts and uncles and girls' hockey teams we view in old photographs: "They have been zapped out of this experience." They have gone on the ultimate spiritual journey, no matter what and how they lived. And we will follow them, each and every one of us.

Yet, as the middle part of the book makes clear, Da Free John is not preaching ascetic detachment from a world of illusions. To flee life through forced deprivation is just another self-imposed trap. Experience in this world can be joyful and enlightening as long as one sees it for what it is, and gives it back to God. In fact, we *must* do this, or we deny the Divine Radiant Presence in the world: "You believe that the Divine is some *One* else or Other. You think that the Divine is so profound you could not Realize God except in a totally different state, circumstance, and dimension than this present one. But God is simply the Shining, Conscious Being That is our Nature at all Times and under all circumstances."

Da Free John is extraordinarily thorough in his lists of false assurances — things we tell ourselves that will make no difference in the end. Even reading the book and accepting its words will not save us, for it becomes just another experience of knowledge in a situation in which knowledge is not the answer. The Universe does not want our belief or our promises, and it cannot use our knowledge. The Universe is more profound than culture, thus cannot be subjected to cultural sanction or scientific law. It ignores fact and even quantity; it confounds narrative and logic.

The actual experience of death will overwhelm any planning, any memory. And "the ego has no intention of bringing itself to an end. Ego-death is not the result of something that the ego can do to itself."

The cosmic shock of death will not suddenly enlighten us and make it possible for us to transcend. We should not rely on the inevitable improvement of our insights in a purgatory or heaven, or some vague guess of another chance after reincarnation. "The same mechanics that are effective in life are effective after death, and your ability to transcend them will not be greater than that which you enjoyed in life. . . . You will have no more ability than you have now."

One may nurture the best of intentions for merging with higher planes, but under the actuality of the transition between lives, everyone will be returned inevitably to where they are. The universe has no other way. "No mere belief in Jesus, or God, or any superior power . . . is sufficient to move you into the Transcendental Condition." Despite piety and preparation, you are suddenly distracted by the rush of pain and desire at the heart of your being. A terror of nausea subsumes you in its reality. And you no longer have any of the knowledge you accumulated in life: "You cannot even hold on to your philosophy or your mantra when you pass by a crosslegged nude on a couch! So what do you think happens from life to death and back to life again . . . in the midst of such a profound event as psycho-physical death?"

The answer lies in cultivating attention and full joyful surrender before death. Da Free John's "easy death" is a willing, conscious giving back of life. You surrender not because you give up and are confounded but because you understand that your life was a gift and you must return it. You surrender not because there is nothing left in the end and you are obliterated and extinguished anyway but because there is nothing to keep and the law that has given you life in the beginning requires surrender at its end. "God is the sole owner of everything, even of our relationships."

In this way, death becomes a necessary experience, "a radical fast," Da Free John calls it, since it purifies us of our elemental aspect, our gross self. If we feel there is nothing other than this gross self, that does not reduce our reality; ideas can no more destroy than preserve whatever is our soul. Even if we feel we must be something more, that in itself does not create something more. "Knowledge is never more than knowledge about — and knowledge about is confounded by death. There is no knowledge about things that is senior to death. Death is the transformation of the knower. . . . Death is a process in which the knower is transformed, and all previous or conditional knowing is scrambled or confounded. . . . To consider death is fruitless, since the knower is what is changed by death."

Through the middle and latter parts of the book Da Free John provides methods of practice and tools for understanding. He describes the process of moving through the subtler aspects of the brain and nervous system into the source of mind and phenomena through the mechanics of attention. His teachings are a less mythologized version of *The Tibetan Book of the Dead.* He depicts the Cosmic Mandala that serves as a guide to the dead person, and he presents it from a variety of angles and perspectives. Most notably he reminds his listeners not to wait until they are no longer alive: "Because the Mandala is duplicated in every fraction of all appearances, it can be visualized in the structures of our own brain." The Mandala is present everywhere, but it remains a separated image when attention is attached to this plane.

Toward the very end of the book Da Free John teaches the living how to serve the dying person, how to care for the body, how to facilitate transition, how to overcome the sorrow of the loss of a loved one and surrender him or her to God. Culminating a long case history of the death of a six-year-old, the Master reminds the grieving parents: "He is nobody's son now."

Da Free John closes the book by showing once again that death is simply another experience in life. If one sees life clearly for what it is, then death will not represent a major change at all; it will be simply a relocation, as from California to New Zealand. If life is surrendered before death, it will not have to be surrendered under duress at the time of death.

In a dream we are surrounded by people who are aspects of our own psyche. If we are told by one of them that we are dreaming, we may hear it, but it is part of the chatter of the dream and does not alter our dreaming. During waking life we are also aspects of a dream, but it is the dream of a Radiant Conscious Being. In the dream of this being we are all the same person; thus, there is only one death: all our deaths. "And when you Awaken," Da Free John tells us, "you will Awaken to and *as* the very same Being that I am."

The only thing I can criticize about this book has nothing to do with the talks of Da Free John or the circumstances in which he spoke. There is, however, something very disturbing about the way in which the talks are presented. A series of needless forewords, introductions, and prefaces opens the book and then recurs at the beginning of each new chapter. Nothing particularly wrongheaded or disturbing is said in these fillers, but they are an almost profane distraction from the sheer force of the book. They go on interminably about other systems of death, personal experience of the writers, and Da Free John as religious theology. They strike me as academic posturing and add nothing. Because Da Free John's statements are themselves so complete and lucid, the filler becomes almost self-mockery. The unintentional result of the juxtaposition of text and filler is to refute the filler as indulgent sophistry. I find the problem can be solved simply by skipping this material. It should not dissuade anyone from engaging the real text.

I am equally bothered by the run of quotations on the book's cover. Many fine people speak in praise of Da Free John, but the quotes sound silly in the context of the message of the book. Here is a matter of life and death, presented in chilling absolutism, and then the book itself is decorated with a bunch of congratulatory glosses.

In the pages themselves Da Free John warns us against taking too seriously the spiritual literature on life after death. After all, he points out, people brought back to life from near death give egoic interpretations of states which are essentially non-egoic — in order to reassure themselves that they are going to a peaceful and shining place and will be among loved ones. Yet the book cover is stickered and designed in such a way as to suggest that the book is exactly about such reassuring visions and interpretations.

I believe these are the well-meaning attempts of Da Free John's followers to make his work acceptable to a wider audience and to put him in the mainstream of "New Age" science and religion. But this is a fallacy. Da Free John's value is that he is disturbing and radical. He does not belong in the mainstream of either science or religion and is not one of the new synthesizers. Since he opposes the ego- and career-oriented mysticism of the counterculture, he should not be marketed as a "New Age" product.

1985

LETTER TO
THE MACARTHUR
FOUNDATION

John D. and Catherine MacArthur Foundation
140 S. Dearborn
Chicago, Illinois 60602

September 19, 1986

Director of Grants:

I know little about your method of decision-making for grants, but I assume that you are at least somewhat responsive to public suggestions.

Although I see that you have given grants to many remarkable and deserving individuals, I would like to challenge your record on two points, and also to tell you about two candidates I think are worth your considering. I will try to be plain and direct at the risk of being undiplomatic so that at least my intention is clear.

First of all, I feel that your awarding of a grant to James Randi was more political than substantial. In essence, what you were saying by this award (to my hearing anyway) is: We want to support as strongly as possible the notion that paranormal phenomena do not exist, that those who claim paranormal abilities are frauds and that those who study them are naive dupes.

The award communicates your wish to be regarded publicly

as the strongest possible opponent of paranormal research. No balancing award (that I know of) was given to a highly-regarded paranormal researcher — implying that you don't believe that any exist. In any unbiased situation one would expect to find equal support for both sides of an unresolved and fundamental scientific controversy (but your award suggests that you think this is no controversy, only a fraud that needs exposing). Additionally, you gave your award not to any legitimate recognized scientist but to (essentially) an entertaining craftsman. I do not suggest you should have a bias against crafts, but nothing in the context of the award suggests that you would consider other craftspeople as candidates. Instead, the implication is that you wish to show such contempt for the fields that Mr. Randi is allegedly debunking that you would rather give the honor to him than to a scientist or another artist. It is also general knowledge that Mr. Randi avoids debunking parapsychological experiments that are not easy marks. I know of three cases where he has refused challenges — in fact, refused even to answer correspondence — and these cases involve far more respected parapsychologists and institutions than those he has ostensibly exposed. In one case, Dr. Jule Eisenbud of Denver repeatedly sent him telegrams and offered to match his publicized financial bounty in exchange for his (Randi's) attempt to expose psychic photographer Ted Serios. Randi's response to those telegrams (or lack of it) suggests very much a boxer picking opponents for appearance's sake. I assume that you researched Randi's credentials thoroughly, so I am baffled as to why his repeated failures to respond to serious challenges were not judged as evidence of a biased researcher and also of a far more limited talent than the award would seem to require. I do not have firsthand access to these exchanges, so I am willing to accept that there might have been extenuating circumstances. However, this negative opinion of Randi's motives and character is so general and widespread, even among confirmed cynics, that unless there were extenuating circumstances, it would seem that you could have found a more appropriate anti-paranormal researcher, perhaps even (if the cynical point of view holds) a better magician. Instead, it appears that you chose to make a political statement.

But why make such a pessimistic statement? The so-called paranormal covers an area of research so wide as to be virtually undefinable, including scientists with very different methods and goals. Of course, "paranormal" is a misnomer; it merely categorizes the investigation of various phenomena that do not fit into the chosen territories of the present scientific establishment. Some of the research may eventually establish that whole territories are fruitless, but at the same time this area of investigation raises fundamental questions about the history and philosophy of science — questions of epistemology — and may lead to discoveries that will change our view of nature and give us a larger repertoire from which to try to solve our present crises.

The professional scientistic attack upon such research seems to me at very least misanthropic and at worst selfish and egocentric — as if it were more important to protect one's preserve than to discover new categories and directions. It may be that the human race will not survive its present set of dilemmas; in any case, we will have a difficult time, and any possible resources should be explored. Why shouldn't the role of a foundation like yours be to support the possible expansion and transformation of human knowledge and belief (even at the risk of being caught like the emperor with no clothes) rather than to promote parochial territorialism? I am not sure I see the point of an organization with such resources as yours using those resources to support cynicism and careerism. These have plenty of support already and truly do not need your help. Your help is really needed in encouraging new institutions emerging in our midst and in discovering new directions hidden and unexamined within our present stalemates. That is a far more desperate and risky undertaking but a far more heroic one. It may also lead nowhere, but at least it has a chance, while giving awards to the Randis of the world is *certain* to lead nowhere.

I will take this one step further: If your constituency is liberal progressive evolutionary science, then their present most dangerous enemy is the anti-scientific creationist religious right. I feel that the healthiest and ultimately most effective counterattack is an expansion of science, not willy-nilly into questionable areas, but

through a revision of the scope and texture of the inquiry itself
(for instance, a reexamination of the tenets of vitalism in the context of the history of science). In fact, the religious right is cor-
rectly (albeit for the wrong reasons) challenging an arrogance,
rigidity, and protectionism in science. The so-called Amazing
Randi is merely a hitman for those invested, economically and
politically, in the status quo.

My second objection is brief and, in a sense, just an addendum
to the above. In some cases (where I know the people involved)
I feel you have given awards to well-connected academic achievers
who represent little more than a successful adherence to the party
line of their disciplines. They are not particularly brilliant or insightful and are not likely to contribute much to discovery or
transformation. I feel this is the inevitable by-product of the
nepotism within any process of grant-giving: Unfortunately, too
many people are inclined to give awards to their friends and col-
leagues. I think, in any case, it is legitimate to ask for the impossible—that you find objective panelists whose main concern is the
individuation and survival of the human race.

Perhaps most importantly, I would like to recommend two
candidates. I am not unbiased. I know both people and have
published them, but I presume your process of selectivity is such
that you can work through that bias and get an accurate outside
assessment of both.

The first is John Todd, founder of the New Alchemy Institute
on Cape Cod and present director of Ocean Arks and Company
of Stewards in Falmouth, Massachusetts. Todd seems to me the
prototype for whom this award was established. He has given his
life to developing self-sustaining, restorative ecological designs and
technologies. At no profit to himself, taking out no patents, he
has spent years working on these systems with bare resources either
for his work or personal livelihood. Many of his designs are explicitly intended to benefit Third World people in particular crises,
such as reversing the spread of deserts, protecting and expanding
forests and gardens, and developing fishing methods not dependent on petroleum. He has emphasized designs which will last for

centuries if not millennia. His academic work includes agriculture, parasitology, marine biology, tropical medicine, and animal behavior. Given resources to work with, John Todd should come up with radical and unique inventions that will make life better for hundreds of thousands or even millions of people.

The second person is Richard Strozzi Heckler, a psychologist and aikidoist living and working in Petaluma, California. Heckler is the co-founder of the Lomi School, which is an innovative therapeutic institution combining methods from psychotherapy, yoga, the martial arts, Feldenkrais work, and other "psychosomatic" treatments. Lomi School seems more fundamental and tough-minded than its forerunner Esalen, and it has now been running programs for more than a decade. Heckler is particularly noted for his work with juvenile delinquents and gangs in Oakland, where he functions as a therapeutic martial artist. His practice of aikido has enabled him to reach alienated street kids who respect the "fight" as the only resolution of conflict. He can take them through actual combat to the impulse behind battle. Understanding why they fight and how it is different from presumptions, they have a choice, they are able to change.

During the last year (through Sportsmind, a firm in Seattle) he has served as a practicing consultant for the Special Forces of the U.S. Army at Fort Devins, Massachusetts. He has trained with Green Beret troops on a day-to-day basis, teaching them aikido and meditation and exploring the moral and ethical basis of true warriorship. In that pursuit he is continuing the work of the mythical First Earth Battalion, whose role has been to transform the global military into something that protects the planet. By teaching men who have already chosen careers of service and discipline (rather than militaristic or anti-militaristic ideologues), he has one advantage: he can emphasize the *practical* steps necessary to become real protectors. The men understand rigor and exercise already, and they have experienced firsthand the devastation of violence. "I dream," says Heckler, "of a sword that cuts things together."

Instead of operating as a theoretical pacifist, time and time again he has gone into the belly of the beast, merging his own development as a therapist and martial artist with the needs of the community. Down the road he hopes to find bridges between traditional warriors of both the American and Soviet militaries, ultimately teaching aikido and meditation in Russia. He has regularly used his training and skill to create realistic avenues of peacemaking, to transform the human psyche at the point where it is closest to war. He is one of the few people who has discovered a path for using the energies of fighting to create stable institutions and community-oriented processes.

My point of view may not be yours, but I would at least like to advance the argument that people like Todd and Heckler are more appropriate grantees than safe and well-funded academics (or at least equally deserving of consideration). I think you should be examining far more unpredictable and radical people and that some should be surviving the scrutiny.

1986

THE FACE ON MARS

foreword to *The Monuments of Mars*
by Richard C. Hoagland

For a reader first discovering these matters, the topic may seem bizarre and obscure. Monuments on Mars? A sphinxlike human face among the craters and sand?

Is this a science-fiction story?

Is this a new attribution to the already-ubiquitous "ancient astronauts?"

In truth, at first glance the Face on Mars seems more like the invocation of a theosophical cult, or a bit of astral sightseeing, than what it is: a concrete object apparently carved from a Martian mesa in precise alignment to the sun and to surrounding structures. The Face and its adjacent "Monuments" are not the imaginings of flying saucer abductees or paintings from the cover of a science-fiction magazine; they are physiographic protuberances photographed by NASA, our American space agency, in 1976, and yet not discerned . . . because they were not supposed to be there, because they would have been too outrageous to believe.

Outrageous even to the New York publisher who first purchased the rights to this book and then tried to reclassify it as science fiction. Finally it was deemed too far out to publish . . . as fiction!

Now it would be foolish for me to tell you that for sure and certain there is an artificially constructed statue of a human face on the surface of Mars, surrounded by the outcroppings of a buried city. I don't know that as a fact, nor does Richard Hoagland. This is, however, a *bona fide* puzzle for us as a culture and as a species to resolve over the next two or three decades.

However, I can say safely that the objects photographed by Viking on the surface of Mars, particularly in the Cydonia region, have many intrinsic characteristics of artifacts that go beyond (and beneath) the mere subjective appearance of a face and a city, and that these characteristics are the outcome not of idle Man-in-the-Moon stargazing but of the scrutiny of experts in a variety of fields after eight years of critical study. As Hoagland himself has said many times—in this book and elsewhere—if these remarkable objects and alignments turn out to be natural features, then they are a trivial waste of time . . . but if they were made by someone, they absolutely cry out for an explanation—and that explanation, whatever it is, will change the human race's sense of its own identity and destiny.

From my own first knowledge of this phenomenon I have realized, with growing respect, that it is the Face itself which weights the "message" so heavily. To discover life on another world would alone be a fantastic event in our human history. But to discover a Face on another world calls into question the very nature of who *we* are. Either our history is different from what we have traditionally assumed, or our biology is, or both are. Another civilization elsewhere can have its own origin and *raison d'etre* without impinging on our separate terrestrial destiny, but the Face is our face, and it *cannot* have an exogenous or trivial explanation. If someone made it, then "they" picked the one object that would absolutely compel us to come there, for "they" have held a mirror up to our entire planet.

From its sudden unexpected appearance on a NASA data-tape, the Face has been the victim of one debunking after another. NASA didn't even give it the respect of looking twice; in the official collective mind, it had to be a mirage. The space agency squandered its major opportunity to go back and re-photograph the site while the on-board cameras were still functioning. At the time, NASA was considered virtually infallible, and its integrity was unchallenged, so the images fell by the wayside.

The first serious papers on the phenomenon, years later, were ridiculed, and their authors were subjected to cruel teasing and unconscionable innuendo about their motives. They still suffer the professional and personal scars of those encounters. The astronomer with the largest lay audience and the widest personal acceptance, Carl Sagan, has spoofingly compared the Face to a variety of mirages in natural objects ranging from hemispheres of the Moon to a tortilla chip.

The press coverage has been uniformly abysmal; occasional tabloid headlines about the "Monkey Man on Mars" and "Lost Martian Civilizations" have served more as confirmations of Sagan et al. than as rebuttals to them in defense of a significant finding at Cydonia. A humanoid visitation from outer space is a territory that Erich Von Daniken has so abused that it can no longer be invoked seriously by other researchers. Von Daniken cried "Wolf!" so loud that we may now be immune to recognizing the artifacts of actual aliens even in the context of compelling evidence. In recent years the Face has even been the butt of uneducated debunking in the countercultural press (as if writers accused of being gullible about everything intend to prove their critical faculty by setting up and knocking down this one straw man).

We are, as a culture, peculiarly immune to the Face on Mars. Perhaps we have seen too many episodes of *Star Trek* and been through too many "Star Wars," "Wars of the Worlds," and "Close Encounters" to appreciate the meaning of actual contact with the "Other." A shocking percentage of the supposedly educated public in the West has little appreciation of, for example, the real distance from here to Mars, or from this Solar System to another star system. The availability of a clever omnipresent technology and super-animation has dulled us to the actual universe. The Industrial Light and Magic Company may enact spectacular special effects for movies, but it has misguided us as to the *actual* effects of gravity and the scale of the stars and planets. (One editor who rejected this manuscript did so because, in her words, we had already sent men to Mars and, if there were a Face there, our astronauts would have reported it. The misconceptions of both fact and scale here boggle the imagination.) If we think about the aliens of Hollywood, or even the scientific reconstructions of PBS, the Face on Mars may seem tame. But in the real night under the actual sky, its possible presence is chilling.

This is not a movie we have already seen.

Richard Hoagland believes that fear as much as indifference keeps us from acknowledging the Face, i.e., from even *confronting* the dilemma of whether it is natural or artificial. Something in our nature doesn't want to "face" ourselves in this way; the reflection, after all, is just as potentially damaging to the rigid priesthood of Western science as it is to the officials of Western religion. If a human face is there on Mars, it blows just about every orthodoxy wide open.

But then maybe we're ready to have everything blown open. As a species we are teetering on the precipice — of an Armageddon war, of the limited resources and fragile biosphere of our world, and, perhaps most significantly (especially if we expect to solve any of these problems), of meaning itself: our values, beliefs, and sense of self have no ground anymore; we drift among stars and atoms we have conceived as drifting aimlessly among one another. The Face is not a cure to all our ills, but it is a signed, sealed, and delivered paradigm shift, out of which a real human transformation may come.

Already the Face suggests some important things: It tells us we may not be alone and our destiny may be tied to the destiny of Others. It tells us that we are one genetic message, culminating in intelligence. (More than a decade ago, photographs from Moon-travelling ships told us that we were one world, one breathing organism and circulatory system without boundaries.) The Face warns us that however we come to its riddle (or oracle) we do so as a species, not as separate warring nations.

The possible confirmation of such an artifact virtually begs for a joint Soviet-American expedition, both to avoid a deadly competition between us and to put the "face-to-face" meeting at the disposition of the whole planet. (In such an undertaking it little matters that the superpowers do not really represent the whole planet and that they will not go as real trusted friends: symbolically, their collaboration would stand for a potential planetary unity and reconciliation, and the men and women on the mission would be true co-workers; sometimes it is most important to act decently without complete faith . . . then faith may follow.)

I am reminded of the letter Hoagland received from a woman after appearing on one radio talk show; she wrote, "In all the years since I realized what nuclear weapons were and to fear them, nothing seemed as though it would be big enough to rival them, not in my lifetime. Now, I know this sounds strange, but this is the first thing that has given me hope . . . the idea that someone would have gone through all that trouble to build this image of us on another planet. I don't know why, but it just might be the antidote."

At another time Hoagland described the Face as perhaps the one droplet of matter into solution needed to precipitate its crystal. A Face on Mars is such an unlikely thing at this stage of our history and in our present crisis that its confirmation could literally crystallize a new form in us perhaps not at once but over many years, even generations. And then of course . . . there is its message . . . its unknown message . . .

It is telling us that we are very, very old. It screams mutely of an event that occurred in this Solar System before the beginning of time. It is instructing us that our human facsimile is the link, the clue. It is drawing us to look closely this time. It hints that the Egyptian Sphinx might be something else entirely. It says, Third Planet, again, and again, and again — by its massive piece of statuary, its lines of sight to the heavens, its angles and universal constants, its redundancies. If it speaks at all (if it is artificial), then it utters slow and didactic syllables, making sure we understand we must alter our sense of who we are.

It is an oracle on another world.

The harder we look the more we see: not ourselves, but our shadow; not civilization but primal intelligence; not only what must have been (once upon a time) but also what must inevitably be again. Here merge King Arthur, the Easter Island heads, Osiris, Quetzalcoatl, and the Dreamtime stones of the Australian Aborigines. Here Mount Rushmore, Mona Lisa, and the skull of Pithecanthropus are bound in a single crypt. Sarcophagus deathmask, mermaid figurehead, wild monkey, coin of Caesar, Jivaro shrunken

skull . . . scale is irrelevant — there is only one biological trail leading back through the mist.

I am reminded of the words I wrote after my first meeting
with this creature:

> When I was driving home, I fiddled with the radio and
> passed an FM station on which, the announcer said, they were
> going to play a very old version of "Silent Night" — how it might
> have sounded as a Germanic dialect of proto-Indo-European
> with tribal instruments. He paused, I turned up the volume.
> Then I heard the bells, the panpipes, the lute . . . and an an-
> cient Christian pre-Christian melody from the snowy north. I
> imagined were-lights, stars . . . Then the words. When I reached
> the driveway, I sat there in the car listening. I opened the en-
> velope and took out the pictures. Then the real oldness of the
> Face struck me — even before the Ice Age, our image in stone,
> on the Martian tundra. The Shroud of Turin was not so wrong.
> For being both human and prehuman, for being stone and sug-
> gesting compassion, sentience, the Face was archetypally Chris-
> tian, bringing our fragmented and warring planet together in
> a single mask, in a unity beyond our history, outside of ordinary
> time. "Silent Night/Holy Night" for sure, but on another world,
> perhaps even another dimension of creation, the deep night in-
> side us as well. The snow . . . and the bells . . . [1]

A little more than a year later now, on the radio Paul Simon
is singing "Graceland": out of South Africa and in an accounting
of our troubled times he still affirms —

"These are the days of miracle and wonder . . . "

The Face is one of the few wild cards in the human deck. Albeit
on a different scale and for different reasons, it has the potential,
like AIDS, like revolution in Africa, like currency crises, and like
new medicines and religions and forces in physics and biology,
the capacity to transform us.

Among the present voices vying for our attention, it is truly (Paul
Simon, again) "the long . . . distance call."

1986

GIVING THEM A NAME

a talk given at the "Angels, Aliens, and
Archetypes" conference

I have no personal experience with UFOs and aliens, but
like the rest of you I am a visitor to a strange and haunting planet.
No matter what else is loose in the cosmos, our inhabitation of
this body, this life, is the first mystery—and one of undiagnosable
profundity.

Why us? Why here?

What next?

In the last century or two, scientists have catalogued us as
insignificant accidents among the infinities of space, taking what
limited satisfaction remains from their goal of mastering the physical parameters of that universe.

But we and they are also protagonists in a shadow play, and
it is not even certain they speak for themselves, let alone for us.
At the deepest level we have another agenda that no one dares
speak of, no one even knows. It is also unclear whether modern
science represents the expression or repression of our most far-
reaching intelligence and powers.

The parapsychologist Jule Eisenbud claims that there are no
UFOs not associated with paranormal mental phenomena. With
all theories of reality still patent pending, he notes, what isn't a
combination of hypnosis, amnesia, and hypermnesis—from mediums flying miles through the air to crash onto séance tables to
multiple personalities speaking ancient languages and deriving

cube roots of twenty-seven figures, to say nothing of a menagerie of ghosts, ouija boards, and spirit possessions?

Fifteen years ago, in an interview with me, Eisenbud suggested that much of our scientific and technological activity was "in some way that I cannot yet comprehend, a defense against . . . other capacities in us that we don't wish to realize. To put it schematically, and simplistically," he said, "and almost absurdly, because we don't wish to realize that we can just kill with our minds, we go through this whole enormous play of killing with such, of overkilling with such overimplementation. . . . It's a caricature of saying: how can I do it with my mind; I need tanks; I need B-52 bombers; I need napalm, and so on. . . . What I'm trying to say is: there must be, I feel, a relationship between this truth, which we will not see, and this absurd burlesque of aggression that goes on all around us."[1]

This conference is entitled "Angels, Aliens, and Archetypes," which is free territory for spirits, visions, and entities from all sources. The list is endless because it encompasses not only a possible kingdom of distinct phenomena but the names and explanations assigned to these phenomena in different cultures and at different periods of history.

Here I would like to focus on the particular theme of celestial UFOs, spaceship-like manifestations in the night sky—to draw our attention back to a simpler time when it was possible to wonder only about the exotic planets on which life evolved, the creatures dispatched from there to explore the universe. Their heyday was not so long ago, sometime in the mid to late fifties, sustained in many ways into the sixties and seventies, and pervasive enough in the early eighties to evoke the mood in the desert at the beginning of *Close Encounters of the Third Kind*.

In early science fiction, tens of thousands of distinct alien beings piloted material yet sublime vehicles through a geography of fireballs, cosmic dust, and sun-stars. Their myths were background to the beeps of our own first Sputnik and Explorer satellites, countdown followed by the slow rise of a rocket ship, a statement of our willingness to go bodily into the mystery that has covered our species since its entry to consciousness. We were rewarded with stunning images of the three-dimensional radiance of our planet, right to the actual dust and stones of the Moon. Through remote eyes we viewed a Martian day, sunrise to sunset, across a boulder-strewn landscape, then luminescent photographs of Saturn, Jupiter, and their moons, some mottled, some covered with ice, at least one fiery and volcanic, one submerged beneath clouds and perhaps harboring oceans.

This is also the universe of radio messages from extraterrestrials to Air Force jets, UFO crashes in Texas, bodies of aliens in the White House vault — into which Spielberg's chandelier spacecraft descends as a chilling reminder of the "once upon a time" yet to be. It is also the universe of blue sky, summer days, windblown seeds, fields of purple and yellow flowers after the rain, birds rising in single dense waves, their cries filling the air with glyphs, layers of cumulus, waves rolling shells, gulls following fishing boats.

This is the only world we know from within, the genesis of our mystery and wonder. It is the world to which the old-fashioned UFOs came as magnificent intruders because it is the world of our own unfathomability. We received these aliens first in our intimations of them, so long evolving in their own biosystems and landscapes, so remote from the Earth that all of their history and biology would be different from ours. They might even include us someday in their interstellar laws and commerce so our dilemmas would fall to a wise and neutral court. Of course, they might also be insectoid, semi-conscious, conquistador, but our imagination of that through countless science-fiction tales merely added to the peril of the vision. Back in the fifties and sixties, when we went UFO-exploring, we were summoning a range of images and emotions from the edge of our existence, but we kept them within the ground of our daily lives.

My intuition is that this universe with its UFOs is now all but dead. We may be telling ourselves these days we're in better shape, on the brink of a whole new consciousness, a hierarchy of dimensions, cosmic convergences, a birthing beyond this physical shell, but so far (as usual), we're our own preachers; we're the ones doing the telling as well as the listening, and this risks the compensating shadow of spiritual inflation. We have seen some of our wisest gurus become so powerful they could only reclaim their souls by enacting petty decadences — molesting young disciples, driving fleets of sacred cars.

I believe we are evolving slowly; I do not think the universe creates souls to obliterate them, but I also do not expect we are going to be pulled pellmell out of our neuroses, romances, and unfinished cities into the dreamtime. And that is no cause for disappointment, for there is a great deal of mystery and subtlety to explore in these bizarre flesh crystals, each of them containing an unconscious cellular history of the Earth.

Isn't it strange that the early manned capsules and 1969 Moonwalk already seem innocent and nostalgic? U.S. space missions, when they begin again, will be on the level of government committees weighing economic and military priorities. Meanwhile, our intrepid visitors in unimaginable vehicles and bodies and costumes have turned into impalpable riddles such that they seem maybe not to have crossed the vast distances among stars nor even to be true aliens.

Not only have they become less benign since animal slaughter, kidnapping, and baby-stealing have been ascribed to them, but they have become less confidently identified with the stars and possible planets of the night sky and more with poltergeists and spontaneous psi phenomena.

For every incident in which a UFO leaves an analyzable relic, there seems to be a trickster event in which, for instance, an alien deposits a chemically conventional pancake in the hands of a startled contactee or delivers a nonsensical message, or in which a sample of extraterrestrial manufacturing disappears from the laboratory, or turns out to be a mundane alloy. Even more disruptive are the cases in which ostensible UFO encounters have been wiped from contactees' memories by post-hypnotic commands and other forms of tampering. In these circumstances we are hardput to claim that any experience of contact, even a simple sighting, is more than a projection or hallucination. We truly do not know enough about ourselves to guess at who "they" are, especially when "they" are unwilling or unable to present themselves through regular diplomatic channels. Clearly the simplicity of the old days of UFOs was our own simplicity, an innocence in our culture, not a simplicity of the phenomenon.

The distinction between spirit and matter has been challenged so extensively that it is now merely situational, and the goblins, ghosts, and disembodied entities of occult science have combined with outer-space UFOs in a muddle of phenomena. Some of those aliens who remain potentially extraterrestrial have been acting out, at best (and I mean "at best" here) grade-B movies, telling us tales about Orion confederacies, about transgalactic wars, celestial migrations, and imperial star systems, or they have been performing elaborate masquerades. And what can we say in behalf of other beings who murder and cut up the sentient creatures of the fields, kidnap and experiment on human beings, and suck babies out of pregnant women? They certainly aren't travelling Buddhists.

A number of factors have contributed to the transformation of the traditional celestial UFO into the multidimensional, metaphysical one, and, like all changes in consciousness, it has occurred mostly on a subliminal level so that we cannot pinpoint the moment of change. In the relatively early days of UFOs, Carl Jung raised the possibility that unidentified lights and shapes we saw in the heavens were actually forms we projected there, alien beings reifying the shadow of our scientific civilization. Before spaceflight, Jung pointed out, flying entities were gods or spirits. Unable to return to a spiritual universe and equally unable to bring peace and well-being to this technological one, we transpose our images and fears into archetypal machines across the tableau of night.

Jung's insights about UFOs were accepted quite widely for many years, even by those who continued to believe in actual spaceships carrying aliens. After all, just because we have projections and even collective hallucinations doesn't mean that there aren't also aliens. The validity of the metaphysical processes generating shamanic jaguars and condors is not affected by the existence of animal ones, and in fact there is an important synchronistic connection between the two that lies at the heart of a universe seamlessly producing creatures through flesh and archetype both.

In recent years Jung's theory has gained new credibility in

a somewhat different guise. The issue now is not so much whether archetypal and real UFOs could coexist as whether there are UFOs that do not come from outer space and are also not pure transpositions of unconscious material, i.e., UFOs that represent materializations of psychic or paraphysical material independent of individual mentation. In such a condition objects and entities are simultaneously concrete and real, psychic and hallucinatory — and we can never tell the difference. This includes the shamanic forms described by Carlos Castaneda and others, possible visitors from other dimensions, from the future, from realms of disembodied mind (including the dead), and, more deviously, channels of psychotronic mind-manipulation and hypnosis with vision implants. The person experiencing an exogenous alien form cannot tell not only if that form is material or psychic but, if it is psychic, whether it is generated inside himself, outside, or both, and, if an implant, whether it is channelled, or cosmic static.

I don't think there is any way out of this dilemma short of the mythical full disclosure by "them" on the White House lawn. And that is not going to resolve the whole riddle of the paradoxical experiences with entities; it is only going to silence the professional debunkers and carve out a certain small part of the territory as explicable in conventional terms, maybe. . . . Because the inventions of our psychic life will go on.

It strikes me, for instance, as odd — though not necessarily incriminating — that the piloters of UFOs have been taking on aspects of our own most disturbing behavior: they are treating sentient beings with precisely the kind of scientific contempt we now exhibit epidemically, carrying out clandestine operations complete with cover stories. They even seem to have picked up the superpowers' repertoire of brainwashing and dirty tricks. In an era of drugs and torture, they have an arsenal second to none. Are they mocking us? Are they reflections of us? And then, are they even all the same aliens?

I am not alone in advancing the idea that perhaps we are dealing with a variety of different phenomena even under the catchall category of space visitors. The crew from the Pleiades seems to have nothing to do with the genetic experimenters and baby-stealers described by Budd Hopkins among others. The former are unintrusive, informative, conventional to the point of *Book of Mormon*-cliché-ed in their cosmic history and politics (sort of like in the "Star Trek" series where everyone speaks English and is acquainted with conventional political systems, and some of the most advanced cultures are organized like interplanetary Aztecs and Egyptians); the frail, almond-eyed biotechnicians are intrusive and tell us nothing — except, as one abductee so eloquently reported, "Yes, we have the right (to treat you this way)."

How could there be two such different cosmic strategies and why are both types of aliens apparently humanoid?; why should we be interfertile with creatures arising in a different biology not even based on DNA (could genetic engineering on a cosmic scale be that good?), and why don't they ever talk to each other and get it straight what they want from us?

There are also many *other* styles of visitors who claim to be from a variety of star systems and such patently uninhabitable planets in this Solar System as Mercury and Uranus, and who also seem to take no cognizance of one another, *or* the Pleiadians, *or* the baby thieves. I should add: *apparently* they are different entities, and *apparently* they don't talk to each other. We might be experiencing the faint and remote ripple of a transdimensional phenomenon, translated into our ken through layers of resistance and symbolic distortions, such as dreams are, hence fragmentary and condensed in the same way. Such UFOs would be harbingers of the depth and subtlety of the creation. In a less optimistic version, though, the explanations we can presently imagine are not reassuring because the aliens come off as mechanically-obsessed, materialistic, not respectful or compassionate of sentient life, sort of like small-time crooks with flashy machines (we've also made up that story many times). We can always argue, as with the old gods, that their ways are not our ways — but I'd rather not give them that honor until we are talking about *bona fide* gods. If you think it's even remotely reassuring that we might be someone else's genetic experiment, you'd better dig deep into the darkest possible nightmares, because there is no salvation there either inside or outside of history, and none in the dharma either.

So let us move away from both the original metallic UFOs and the new psychic and psychotropic ones. Let us consider that we have an original and unassailable integrity because it is on that ground alone that we meet the aliens and on that ground alone that the term "alien" has any meaning. We are led by sweet layers of flesh and psyche, and when we are no longer able to trust them, we become just one more note in a chaos of transgalactic noise— radio, metaphysical, bodily, extrabodily, and other.

When "*It* Came from Outer Space," we were *here*, in our cities and villages, with ordinary hopes and fears. The real Earth, with its immediate sun-star, great seas, and profound mysterious landscapes, is our protector and our solace; it is the source of our psychic and emotional strength. All things meaningful come from our hearts, and in that sense no UFO can be as wondrous as the birth in blood of a single child, or even the birth of a furry mole, the arising by cells of a dragonfly from its egg. The metaphysical UFOs, abductors, maintainers of bases in the Andes, and gener- ators of Bigfeet and Loch Ness monsters are prophetic, but they are also restrictive and authoritarian, if not in themselves, then in the hands of those who interpret them for us; we become re- duced to their unsolved paradigm at the risk of the things that make us real, that define our world as home to which anything else comes from beyond, our lives as worth preserving in the strange and unknown cosmos. That is why the ancient, enormous Sphinx of a human face carved into a Martian mesa has a special signifi- cance even among more intimate and contemporary meetings with aliens. That one we can go out and see in our own spaceships just as we went to the pyramids of Egypt and the temples of Greece. We can touch it in our own terms.

The original ground on which we stand is this world, the familiarity of our body/minds, language, and civilization, however much in crisis that might seem and no matter that we judge our- selves to have made a mess of it. It is still what we are, by karmic law what we have chosen to be, a materialization of our pro- foundest desires. We shouldn't be looking any more for a literal biblical god, or his fundamentalist equivalent in a super alien biologist. There are probably billions of possible manifestations in the universe and we could transmute among them authentically for innumerable lifetimes, all manner of planets and dimensions and subatomic particles. That's not yet our destiny; even unenlightened, we live, experience wondrous things, breed, and die, and we should not stand ready to cede that to aliens, to submit it to their judgment, or to deem them automatically superior to it — not out of false pride but because we exist only as the legitimate outcome of the forces that we express. We cannot be anything else, and I would argue that this is true even if we *are* someone else's experiment — and I will get right to the point on that one: even if we are the genetic experiment of a scientifically advanced race, the experiment can only be a manipulation of existing life forms; it does not include the invention of our whole existence. Our genes can be synthesized, or rearranged; the biological frame of our life can be altered, but biology itself cannot be invented out of nothing by something that is itself an evolutionary product of the universe. Frank Herbert fashioned the genetic priesthood and Tleilaxu flesh tanks, wrote the whole *Dune* series to arrive at this single truth.

If the aliens are biological, to use the term in its broadest trans-DNA sense, then we are biological in the same way, and the experience to which biology refers remains intact. Put another way — genetic manipulation (which is just an intense form of natural selection) may determine what range of phenomena we deal with as organisms, but it cannot invent the original phenomenology, the impulse for something to become in a universe where nothing might as easily have been. That creationary force, operating through intelligent entities or through randomly distributed pools of local planetary starstuff, that archetypal, individuating force (if you prefer) is still going to incarnate creatures at the same level of enlightenment and existence. Our creators are not going to be any more enlightened than we are; they will just have advanced technologies. They know no more about how the universe came to be, why it is, and what anything in it is. Their missions and experiments should not trap us and our civilization in the meanings they give to them and the ostensible goals they set (any more than we can change the existential fact of a genetically-altered rabbit).

If the UFOs contain or *are* authentic evolved beings — and if they mean to compel and even midwife us into our destined maturities — we can still wait for their actual surprise. Nothing said here will prepare us for an experience of them. No one else's account can stand in place of our own ("No one else's hands will ever do," the Stones sang years ago, and also: "Stand up coming years, escalation fears; oh, yes, we will find out. . . ."). There is no reason to leave this conference feeling as though we have to evolve faster in order to fulfill prophecy or respond to the UFO warning. Because the gods have yet to make any rules for us, and I doubt that they are going to change strategies now and simply say, "Be good — or be high." We are far too perverse and unconscious to respond to such a message anyway. Most people don't want to evolve, and won't; they'll scratch and claw their way out of any power trip, however posed in the language of love and beneficence. If need be, they'll vandalize the ships of heaven and spray the gods themselves with graffiti. And they certainly don't want *us* to lead them. But when the real thing arrives, they'll be ready too, and they won't even know it's a UFO. Nor will we.

That is why I am reminding us of the old green and blue Flash Gordon "African Queen" Earth to which the aliens first came, Al Jolson singing "Old Man River," and a thousand other native songs in the air from Siberia to Somalia to Peru. When we are able to meet them there, to be us and let them be them, and they are neither our projections nor our inventors, then the story they tell us, rather than a horror story and the intimation of our own nightmare, is something truly mysterious and from the other end of matter.

1987

A CRITICAL LOOK
AT THE NEW AGE

As long as we exist in this universe, phenomena will bewilder us. The strangeness of our situation is original; it is a strangeness that science dissects and emerges dialectically from. Our occasion ostensibly began with a cataclysmic explosion at the heart of matter, creating time and space and separating the microcosm from the macrocosm. That is the secular interpretation. What preceded this explosion, where it occurred in a realm before time and space, and from whence its tinder originated are *completely outside* the purview of science. Likewise, the best that science can do with our fine inner edge of sentience and rotation (what Arthur Young, the inventor of the Bell Helicopter, calls "angular momentum — the one thing that makes it all go"[1]) is to claim that these too are the refined but happenstance result of chance interactions in the debris.

We don't mean whatever it is we say — so science tells us (or we tell ourselves through science); we *mean* nothing. About our freedom, science says simply: it's not real freedom but an illusion by which robotlike chemical reactions imagine themselves initiating thought and motion. (Sacred science might also deny our free will and assign our acts to stars and deities, but priests of all lineages interpret this dilemma by a deeper and ultimately conscious karma.)

Any event is of course inexplicable in terms of original and final causes, but science subcategorizes its hierarchies of riddles as sets of one another, all going back to the origin of subatomic primes. The elemental chart strips the numerical basis for matter; the atoms it unmasks embody their own ratios and codes. All science is, to one degree or another, quantitative analysis of thermodynamic/gravitational effects governing these materials.

But quantum physics has demonstrated that the forces which lie at the heart of our unfolding do not maintain simple billiard-ball effects. The concrete appearances of our realm are actually forms of radiation, a fact that potentially legitimizes "ghost" effects considered vitalistic or supernatural (and thus imaginary) by science. The enigma of light itself, which is not matter and does not obey the laws of "physical" objects, should be sufficient to dissuade us from overly literal expectations. Arthur Young writes:

"Light is not seen, it is seeing. Even when a photon is partially annihilated, as in scattering of photons by electrons, what remains is not part of the old photon, but a new photon of lower frequency, going in a different direction. . . . A hammer striking a nail exerts a force which drives the nail; a bowling ball conveys energy which knocks over the pins. In both cases, the hammer and the bowling ball remain after the work is done. With light, however, its transport of energy from one point to another leaves no residue. *Light is pure action*, unattached to any object, like the smile without the cat."[2]

Such a reprieve is significant not so much for opening a frontier but in drawing our inquiries back to the phenomenological universe we already inhabit.

In a 1983 exchange with his students (about the coevolution of flowers and bees) Da Free John challenged the Darwinian proposition of chance and form:

"[A flower] may have been red by chance, but how did it get to be seen by chance? How did it enter into the realm of being seen?

". . . . It is obvious to me that Nature is made of consciousness. It is made of Conscious Force. All of this apparently inert matter is Conscious Energy. It appears to be objective to us because we are already objectified, discrete entities, functioning in relation to these forms. But if we were to transcend ourselves and enter into the Source of our own existence, we would discover that all of this objective, material, solid Nature is Conscious Energy. . . .

". . . . Everything in nature is an expression of both Energy and Consciousness. Everything in Nature is, mysteriously, completely known somehow. Every flower that grows arises within an infinite Domain of Consciousness and Energy, which is full of Wisdom, bizarre and marvelous, and which makes it possible for all kinds of cooperative organisms to appear and for beings such as ourselves to arise. . . .

". . . . How could something come to be by chance if there is nothing to begin with? How can there be anything like chance to begin with? Why is there anything? How can there be something rather than nothing? Why should there be something if all there is is mechanical chance in Nature? Why should there be Nature to begin with? You cannot have nothing to begin with and then have the existence of something be based on chance. The existence of something rather than nothing is the expression of a mystery that goes far beyond mechanical probability."[3]

This mystery is impenetrable by science, for science is simply a naturalist reduction, a pretence that our lives can objectify their own being.

While cataloguing the myths of ancient and tribal peoples, the anthropologist Claude Lévi-Strauss points out the fallacy of treating every etiology as if it were either putative natural history or a failed attempt to explain the inexplicable. It is not nature which is inexplicable, but ourselves. Our ancestors did not invent myths one by one to resolve each new paradox. We have been inexplicable all along—in our shape and means of birth, in our relationships to one another and to other species, in our manner of cooking and eating food, in our divisions into clans and nations, in our customs and taboos, in our deaths. By the time any discrete event occurs, our myth-making process seizes the opportunity mostly in order to explain *itself*:

". . . . Natural conditions are not just passively accepted. What is more they do not exist in their own right for they are a function of the techniques and way of life of the people who define and give them meaning by developing them in a particular direction. Nature is not itself contradictory. It can become so only in terms of some specific human activity which takes part in it . . . "

This is perhaps chic academic jargon, but he is talking about whence meaning arises. Meaning does not originate externally (unless we want to give that power to archetypes). Meaning arises solely through our relationships.

" . . . Even when raised to that human level which alone can make them intelligible, man's relations with his natural environment remain objects of thought: man never perceives them passively; having reduced them to concepts, he compounds them in order to arrive at a system which is never determined in advance. . . . The mistake of . . . the Naturalist School was to think that natural phenomena are *what* myths seek to explain [and we can include science or any New-Age paraphysics among these myths], when they [phenomena] are rather the *medium through which* myths try to explain facts which are themselves not of a natural but a logical order."[4]

I would quibble with the use of the word "logical" here; Lévi-Strauss is basically a debunker of the supernatural sources of totemic and shamanic knowledge. But his underlying argument stands: there is no simple link of explanation between natural phenomena and their descriptions, whether those phenomena be rainbows and thunderstorms or synchronicities and UFOs.

Seemingly "psychological" aberrations are really part of an undeclared branch of physics: As much as quantum physics — though in a different way — they point to the breakdown of the billiard-ball theory of reality and its prerequisite Big-Bang Universe. Paraphysics is their better name.

Extraordinary events — of healing, of astrological coincidence, of seemingly impossible transfers of information and substance — by the sheer fact that they occur are crucial to a "consciousness" model of reality. They do not portend a New Age but have proceeded from the beginning of time; in fact, present New-Age wonders are a mere glimmering of what creatures in our lineage have glimpsed.

Parapsychology has been the single forum for scientific analysis of these incidents. Objects dislodged seemingly by thought, pictures forming on film in the context of mental phenomena, apperceptions of future events, levitation, incorruptible corpses, out-of-the-body "dreams," and apparent transfer of information between minds — have all occurred in laboratory settings. Engineers, physicists, psychologists, medical doctors, and even stage magicians have attended these sessions, but, interestingly, the real issues have never breached mainstream scientific dialogue because there is no place even for their consideration. Witness Jacques Benveniste's recent attempt to test the "memory" of water molecules in a homoeopathic context. His experiment confirming the biological activity of microdoses was published by *Nature* with their own embarrassed proviso that the results were without physical basis. As quickly as feasible the editors then sent their own goons (including stage-magician James Randi) to Benveniste's laboratory who "officially" refuted the prior results. This is hardly science attempting to explore the unknown; it is science policing orthodoxy.

Objectified analysis is the contemporary engine of mythogenesis. Although the institution of science supposedly seeks a comprehensive theory for reality, individual scientists tend to limit their research to those areas that fit theories they have already developed and to ignore ones that challenge the basic meaning of that work. They may suffer, obscurely, the daunting scale and emptiness of their cosmology, but at least they control the mechanical effects of its universe, which submit to their formulas. The parapsychologist Jule Eisenbud has rightly observed that all their declarations are patent pending until paranormal events are explained.

In his recent book *Afterlife* Colin Wilson describes at length the performances of mediums throughout the nineteenth and early twentieth century. During carefully documented sessions attended by practicing skeptics (even then), musical instruments materialized and played in the air, people rose straight up off the ground without any contrivances, exotically-clothed entities paraded through rooms, and "psychics" divulged remarkable information unavailable to them by ordinary means.

At one point Wilson describes the feats of an enormous young medium named Agnes Nichols who practiced in the 1860s and 1870s; she was deemed capable of generating apports, that is, material objects that dropped out of thin air. When Alfred Russel Wallace (of Darwin-and-Wallace evolution theory) "asked her if the spirits could produce a sunflower, a six-foot sunflower with a clod of earth around its roots fell on to the table." Patent pending indeed! (As I read that passage I imagine the last crumbs of no doubt molecularly ordinary earth spilling onto the floor.)

"Agnes' spirits never did things by halves; on another occasion when someone requested flowers, what looked like the whole contents of a flower shop cascaded from the air. But their most spectacular feat occurred in 1871 when Agnes herself (now married to a man called Guppy) became the 'apport'. She was seated at the dining-room table doing her accounts when she vanished as if the ground had swallowed her. Four miles away, some ardent spiritualists were seated at a table with their eyes closed, begging the spirits to vouchsafe some small manifestation. There was an almighty crash that caused screams, and when someone struck a match, the mountainous Mrs. Guppy was found lying on the table, still clutching her account book."[5]

If true as reported, this would be one more instance that the "spirits" do not lack a sense of humor.

Wilson writing on survival outside the physical body, Jacques Vallee expounding on UFOs (*The Invisible College*), Robert Munroe describing the varieties of experience traditionally known as astral projection (*Far Journeys*) all tackle roughly the same body of information. These realms and their entities represent an unknown manifestation of such a diverse nature as to defy any categorization even within the traditional occult. They are neither physical nor mental as we ordinarily make these distinctions. For instance, ordinary people (housewives and policemen) have discovered only under hypnosis that they were abducted for alien experiments — episodes that have been subliminally suppressed by abductors whose frail appearance and erratic, unskillful behavior do not encourage any model of advanced extraterrestrials. Other — seemingly celestial — aliens arrive aboard UFOs in the guise of trolls from ancient Ireland, while, in the American Northwest, their counterparts merge with the uncapturable yeti. Are these *their* masks or *our* projections?

Let me cite another series of episodes from Wilson, of a somewhat different nature:

"A five-year-old boy, Benjamin Blyth, was out walking with his father, and asked him what time it was; his father said it was half past seven. A few minutes later the child said: 'In that case I have been alive . . . ', and named the exact number of seconds since his birth. When they got home, his father took a sheet of paper and worked it out. 'You made a mistake — you were wrong by 172,800 seconds.' 'No, I wasn't,' said the child, 'you forgot the two leap years, 1820 and 1824.'. . . .

"A modern case can illustrate more clearly what is at issue: the 'calendar calculating twins' John and Michael, 'idiot savants' who have spent most of their lives in a state mental hospital in America. They have been described by the psychiatrist Oliver Sacks. Although the twins are mentally subnormal, with an IQ of only sixty, they can name the day of the week of any date in the past or future forty thousand years. Asked, let us say, about 6 March 1877, they shout almost instantly: 'Tuesday.' And they have no more difficulty about a date long before the Great Pyramid was built. Yet, oddly enough, the twins have the utmost difficulty with ordinary addition and subtraction, and do not appear to even understand multiplication and division. . . . [Dr. Sacks] was present one day when a box of matches fell on the floor, and both twins said immediately: 'A hundred and eleven.' When Sacks counted the matches, there were, indeed, a hundred and eleven. The twins also murmured 'Thirty-seven', and when Sacks asked them why, they explained that three thirty-sevens make a hundred and eleven. He asked them how they knew there were a hundred and eleven. 'We *saw* it.' . . .

"On another occasion, Sacks walked up behind them when they were repeating numbers to one another. One would say a six-figure number, and the other would savour it, then say another six-figure number. Sacks made a note of these numbers, and when he got home, studied them carefully. He discovered that they were all prime numbers—numbers that cannot be divided exactly by any other number . . .

" . . . There is no short cut to finding out whether some huge number *is* a prime, except by painstakingly dividing every other number into it (Sacks used a book.)

"How were the twins doing it? They could not be calculating them—they had virtually no power of calculation. The next day, Sacks went to see them carrying his book on prime numbers. They were still playing the number game, and Sacks joined in, repeating an *eight*-figure prime. There was a half-minute pause while they looked at him in astonishment, then both broke into smiles, and began swapping eight-figure primes. An hour later they were swapping twenty-four-figure primes—although even an 'electronic brain' would take some time to work out whether such a huge figure is a prime or not."[6]

Wilson offers a theory based on alternating hemispheres of the brain and multiple personalities, but we don't require theories in order to appreciate occurrences. We can always dream up cosmologies which 'explain' phenomena, but none of them capture our sheer wonder and disorientation—let alone the pure ongoing magic of starry heavens and purple clover.

UFO literature is a book of riddles and conundrums. Beings of reputedly remote origin reach us through both mediums and spacecraft; at least "they" say the same things through these very different channels. The messages may suddenly interrupt ordinary radio transmissions, assemble themselves through table tapping, or get delivered in sealed envelopes by humanoids debarking from toruses. Their content suggests ordinary theosophy or science fiction: "We have passed our souls, bodies, and minds into computers and moved several of millions of light-years backwards toward your time and dimension"; "A cosmic morality such as the one we share forbids us to intervene"; "We will return to see you two more times"; "We believe in the Almighty Power of the Universe. You must understand that there are over 150 billion universes, and that there are many forms and orders of Gods in each and every one of them"; "We will harmonize this world with the rest of the universe"; "Rentre dans ton silence et souffle tes chandelles"; and so on.[7]

Even celestial UFOs do not have to be metallic ships; they can manifest as the Holy Virgin Mary, Khidr the Sufi angel, or a Hopi blue kachina. Vallee describes the initial sighting at Fatima:

"The first apparition of the woman took place on May 13, 1917. Three children were watching their sheep when a bright flash surprised them, and they walked toward the large hollow pasture called Cova da Iria . . . to see what had happened. They found themselves caught in a glowing light that almost blinded them, and in the center of the light they perceived a little woman, who spoke to them, begging them to return every month to the same spot. . . .

"On August 13 there were eighteen thousand people at the site of the apparitions. . . . A clap of thunder was heard, followed by a bright flash. A small whitish cloud was forming around the tree. It hovered for a few minutes, then rose and melted away. The clouds in the sky had turned crimson red, and then changed to pink, yellow, and blue. 'Colored light like a rainbow on the ground'; clouds around the sun reflecting different colors on the people' — such are some of the terms the witnesses used to describe it. The witnesses saw 'falling flowers,' the famous phenomenon of 'angel hair' so consistently reported after the passage of a UFO, and sometimes interpreted as an ionization effect. One man, Manuel Pedro Marto, reported seeing clearly *a luminous globe spinning through the clouds. . . .* "[8]

At subsequent visitations through October 13, the crowd gradually swelled to seventy thousand; there were flashes of light, a sudden end to heavy rain, rainbow-colored disks that doused the throng in lights, sweet aromas, spontaneous healings, the manifestation of a "Lady" who introduced herself as the Angel of Peace, then the delivery of a communiqué to be read in 1960. Vallee adds:

"A man whose word I trust received an interesting report from one of the Pope's secretaries, who introduced the highest men in the Church into the presence of John XXIII for the opening of the secret part of the Fatima prophecy in 1960. Although the

solemn event took place behind closed doors, the secretary had
the opportunity to see the cardinals as they left the Pope's office;
they had a look of deep horror on their faces. He got up from
behind his desk and tried to speak to one of them whom he knew
intimately, but the prelate gently pushed him aside and walked
on with the expression of someone who has seen a ghost."[9]

This probably means that the message was little different from
those received by 1950s Air Force pilots whose radio channels were
coopted, for instance, with descriptions of beings who live on the
interior of Saturn and prophecies of the Earth entering the Fourth
Dimension with an uprising of Atlantis in the Bermuda Triangle.
(The deadlines for all of these have long since passed.)

An institution based on interpreting exogenous messages must
suffer the literalism of both the carrier and the text. *The Book
of Mormon, Oahspe,* and *The Book of Urantia* are all the products of such originless transmission. The notion of the immaculate
Son of God has mostly time and tradition behind it to separate
it from more garish visitations: Jesus can no longer be debunked
by a panel of experts. But once the Church is lured into a contemporary interaction with mediums and UFOs, it too becomes
part of the grand unresolved science-fiction conspiracy and rests
on the same footing as any other paraphysical cult.

Until the Martians appear on the White House lawn we must
treat the whole phenomenon (including reincarnation) not as
natural history of the cosmos but one of the mysteries arising from
our existence.

Because of our rock video/soap opera mentality we are seduced
by a melodramatic, inflated interpretation of what is happening
to us. Certainly the 'big event' in which we all exist is unfolding
today as it always was, but it is not intrinsically more apocalyptic now, either in the positive or negative sense. To the degree
that some critical moment is precipitating, it is not likely to be
the one we are heralding anyway. Cosmic epochs, communications with disembodied entities, realms of astral travel, etc., still
await determination. They cannot be simultaneously experienced,
described, decoded, and marketed. The much heralded Harmonic

Convergence impersonates another visitor to our region fifteen years earlier (I think even the most committed believers must sense by now that they are the targets of the packaging of an image rather than the visitation itself):

"PAGAN FESTIVAL OF THE COMET KAHOUTEK

"The comet Kahoutek is much more than a cloud of interstellar dust. It is a psychic energy wave that travels through the cosmos in four dimensions. Its passage across our heavens has outstanding significance for mankind. THIS IS OUR BIG CHANCE. Each of our brains contains long neglected primal sensory apparatus that links us directly to the comet. We can *re-awaken* these senses and tune in on *comet power*. Certain mutant earthlings, through the grace of God, find themselves already in contact with Kahoutek. The energy that flows from the comet is more powerful than nuclear energy. This is the solution to the energy crisis! We are gathering together a vast assembly of mutants, all with exceptional abilities to transfuse comet power. We will tune in on the comet. We will absorb the primal energies into our bodies and rebroadcast them into our *psychic energy accumulator*. Our psychic energy accumulator stores comet power, like a battery, for use as fuel. A prototype-unit will be on display and ready to take on its first charge on Saturday."—Psychic Energy Storage Depot, Springfield, Illinois.

This flyer states with almost painful explicitness our original New Age dilemma. By comparison Harmonic Convergence seems like decadent post-Prince styling.

[Ten years ago in Vermont the left-wing anarchist writer Murray Bookchin was joking with me about 'California Dumb,' as he called it. 'California Dumb' I took to be the belief that what was unfolding in California was happening for the first time in the history of the planet and represented an absolute breakthrough in human consciousness (Murray was particularly upset at Governor Jerry Brown and his associates for their ecological faddism and lack of global-political savvy). However, I remembered that when Murray first visited The New Alchemy Institute in Cape Cod, an alternative-energy center he had praised widely in epochal

terms, he left quickly and checked into a Howard Johnson's in
order to be able to smoke cigarettes and eat junkfood (Jerry Brown
later went to India to feed and bathe the poor). So I reminded
Murray there was also a 'New York Dumb'. He asked what that
was, and I said, "The belief that you can just say it and give
speeches about it and don't have to do it."

"Then I'm New York Dumb," he said defiantly, "and proud
of it."

Hopefully we walk the precipice between those two.]

All our lives we are the recipients of messages even if these messages
(like dreams) turn out to be from the depths of our own beings.
From one standpoint our own depth and the depth of the universe — at least the signified universe — must be the same. A primary cause of New Age confusion is that we cannot *ever* tell the
difference between ostensible voices of aliens who evolved far from
here and voices of the Earth (be those our own unconscious selves,
telepathic transmissions from the minds of fellow humans, or chan-
nellings from so-called other dimensions or the dead). In fact, as
much as we know (and it is not really very much) about the shape
of the three-dimensional universe, we know almost nothing about
the topology of consciousness, so when someone like the famed
astral traveller Robert Munroe reports on meetings with entities
who have gotten sidetracked on the Earth, we cannot tell if these
are terrestrially-created intelligences (perhaps from his own mul-
tiple-personality, story-telling potential, perhaps from shamanic
entities), or if they are authentic visitors who arose indigenously
in their geospheres and travelled here. As long as we entertain the
notion of intrinsic identity separate of embodiment we also cannot tell the difference between entities who never had "bodies"
(at least in our three-dimensional sense of them), entities who are
permanently disincarnate, and entities who (like Munroe) are tem-
porarily travelling out-of-flesh.

If a minor hypnotic trance causes someone to believe that the
chair on which he is sitting does not exist, that the raisin in his
mouth is a grapefruit, that he was once married to the Queen of
England, what major occurrence is likewise unfolding, unnoticed,

before our noses? If the vast caul of light we are wrapped in is a chimera (within a mirage), what progression of aliases does it mask?

Jule Eisenbud has reviewed a variety of cases in which mediums have served as apparent channels for the personalities of disembodied spirits, including the 1917 reappearance of the notorious eighteenth-century mason Alessandro Cagliostro. Here Eisenbud demonstrates that the agency involved was not necessarily the enduring manifestation of the personality of Cagliostro (or Napoleon, or some Cro-Magnon shaman in other instances) but a displacement through the personality of the medium herself. After concluding that the medium was not enacting the spirit of the dead Cagliostro, he reviews her performance by other criteria:

" . . . This is precisely what mediumship—and mind—are all about. To imagine that Mrs. Chenoweth needed special paranormal cognitive and organizing powers that could have been achieved only through some improbable-unless-proved-otherwise something called super-ESP (plus perhaps the mind of a Shakespeare) is to misread completely everything that is known about plain run-of-the-mill ESP, ESP in everyday life, unconscious ESP in dreams. . . . The notion of super-ESP [and we might add: super-UFOs] is a fiction derived from the feeble glimmers of this latently omniscient and omnipotent faculty seen in the laboratory; and this is, when all is said, just super-nonsense, just another example of the extreme difficulty some persons have in untethering their minds, when thinking and theorizing about psi, from the physical world and its constraints. The only thing that counts where unconscious ESP is concerned—and all forms of psi, for that matter—is meaningfulness, not time, distance, complexity, or anything else. The prime requisite for this is simply unconscious need, not the mental equivalent of the muscles of a weightlifter." [10]

It's meaningfulness that holds together ordinary life; it's meaningfulness that rules reason. And it's meaningfulness, as represented in the great wishfulfillment dream of desire, that brings life itself into being through the sex cells, through libido transformed in eros. The universe is not handed us on a silver platter. It arises, in matters of the mind and soul, only through necessity; in matters of the body, only through instinct. It is desire — neurotic and transcendent, animal and spiritual — through which we make our connection to the cosmos, and this includes our connection to paranormal phenomena and religion. Desire must even lie at the heart of yoga. What validates meditation, zen, and other disciplines is that they will not take our psychospiritual clichés and babble at face value, as if we were neutral recipients of information. Even the most accomplished psychics and mediums must contact the supernatural through their needs, their processes of individuation, the one unique and ineffable point of contact they have with the universe.

Which is why great artists and poets give us a more sublime sense of the gods than the most powerful medium or psychic adventurer. It doesn't take the mental equivalent of a weight-lifter. It doesn't take a New Age or psi phenomena to open us to the wonder and peril of the universe. That's been there all along. If there's anything worth selling as New Age, it's to peer through the bias of materialistic and scientistic culture to see the creation fresh again.

Unfortunately, the most popular New-Age stuff continues to be very Fundamentalist, whether evangelical, right-wing apocalyptic, or New-Age liberal with pop-psychology overtones. The susceptibility of our culture to the Harmonic Convergence was astonishing, especially insofar as it occurred during an era of unprecedented cynicism and amorality. While stage magicians and professional skeptics collaborate to prove that there is no spirit or vital energy in the universe and while greed, punk, and general hardass cruelty are newly honored as virtues from South Africa to Afghanistan to the freeways of L.A., collective religious gullibility is epidemic. People want to believe that the universe is written out linearly and that its great cycles will show themselves and rush to a climax right in our own lifetimes. From transits of Pluto to hieroglyphs on the moon Miranda of Uranus it is a sweet optimism. But it is also naive, and it denies an unprecedented epidemic of genocide and the nuclear flashpoint we live under. Sometimes the New-

Age clichés (whether confirmed by Ramtha et al. or promoted as Mayan or Hopi prophecy) seem to reflect the same ambition to make an easy strike as Insider Trading. It's like someone on Madison Avenue saying, "What! Superstar God won't endorse our product. Well, then get someone else to channel for him."

Santa Cruz rock musician Rob Brezsny leads us right to the Trojan horse:

"The Government, the Government is here inside me now.

"The Government invades my dreams with telepathy, sorcery, World War Harmony,

"But I am unafraid.

"The President, President God Himself, or the Secretary of Blood, or the Undersecretary of World War Harmony, or the Nethersecretary of invading my dreams with nightmare telepathy,

"Their totalitarian love spells purify my sleeptalk. . . . "[11]

Why would the dead linger anyway, to tell us what we already know? As Doris Lessing points out, it is not prophecy we need now; we live in a World Age when everyone is Cassandra, everyone knows what will happen if we continue destroying species of plants and animals and rain forests, washing off topsoil, pouring tons of chemicals into the atmosphere, building nuclear weapons; what we need to know is why no one will listen to us, not even ourselves.[12]

Meanwhile, we are swamped with distractions, passing from cradle to grave in a television-automobile trance, so we are also better off using a longstanding tradition, like Buddhism, to sort angels and destinies than accepting the newest guru or medium on the block; the latter might be susceptible to not only exotic hallucinations but also the metaphors and connotations of pop culture: science fiction, comic books, evangelism, and new science. The older the training the more experience its lineage has with mirages and psychological inflation. Those who reach for the stars (including some of the more accomplished gurus of our time) often cast the darkest, deadliest shadows from their residual humanity.

Christian dogmatic religions also fail their devotees. But it is not the teaching of Jesus that is lacking: It is the literal advocacy

of the *Bible*. Fundamentalism is *always* wrong because the universe
is not literal and not explicit — at least in the languages we speak
(this is true even for the highest mathematics). Channelled messages are no different. Any holy dictated book or UFO transmission or telepathic wisdom from beyond is subject to the same
benighted Fundamentalism. Until we know how to recognize God,
The Word of God is basically the Word of Them — i.e., those who
claim to know more than we do or whose message has to be taken
literally because it's dictated from a higher source. You can have
any kind of Fundamentalism: channelled-message Fundamentalism, Seth-material Fundamentalism, Shirley-MacLaine Fundamentalism. Every UFO message is potentially its own religion.
The visions at Fatima and Lourdes lent themselves to New-Tes-
tament interpretation because the Virgin Mary was the sacred
woman honored there; the people were not going to blaspheme
such a powerful manifestation by suggesting it could be anyone
else.

Robert Munroe's travels on the astral plane (or out-of-the
body, as he prefers) present a related problem. Through an externally induced change in brainwave patterns he leaves his physical self and enters another scenery. Journeying freely there, he
views the dead still attached to this plane, even hovering over 42nd
Street, ghosts that pass right through the pedestrians they grab
at. He comes upon a kind of Dante's Hell — piles of astral bodies
attempting frustrated sex without flesh. He travels into a universe
that dwarfs this one; there he finds zones of beings from other
dimensions, other cosmoses, mining our emotions, deriving from
our energy a kind of celestial food.

He also reports on alternate lives led by different aspects of
ourselves, alternate futures in which the Earth occurs. All this is
ostensibly available to any of us just by closing our eyes, as it were,
and submitting to computer-generated resonance between the
hemispheres of our brain. [13]

But his encounters also suspiciously replicate science-fiction
plots and reveal a mechanical cosmology, with elements of early
twentieth-century surrealism. His neologisms are such mixtures
of airplane jargon and spiritual macho that they suggest another

attempt by the technocrats to take over the universe. (So much for unchecked paraphysics!)

Once again, our difficulty is not with the landscape (which is breathtaking and exhilarating as Munroe describes it) but with his interpretation and ontology. If it is so easy to objectify this whole incarnate existence and then bust out on brainwaves into limitless astral space, not only are we wasting our time with virtually every other activity, but traditional religions have been making the very simple very difficult and the major tenets of philosophy and science are suddenly vacuous.

Perhaps Munroe is right, but it would seem more likely that we are going to find ourselves always looking through one mirage into another.

The tendency to find synchronistic significance in all occurrences distorts a larger truth: There *are* no coincidences on the Moon, C. S. Lewis once reminded us. Either everything has meaning, or nothing has. . . .

New Age seekers, hoping to empower every event by assuming assignations in other lifetimes, or a spirit- and higher entity guided life, turn the possibility of everything having meaning into all the meanings being redundant. The meaning that attends everything only makes sense when we also allow for the billardball universe within its own realm — the random sociology of particles (and humanoids); otherwise, the freedom our condition has earned us becomes meaningless, and we have traded in Newtonian robotic bodies for angelic-controlled bodies: all that changes are the language and teleology of the control.

In the end we are driven back to leading our surprising and ordinary lives much as we were before either the scientists or the New Age enthusiasts intervened — because, in any case, this realm wouldn't (and couldn't) exist unless it expressed the potentialities and consequences at this stage of the universe's development. Enlightenment is possible, but it does not come simply from changing the channel.

Nowadays we are particularly susceptible to reincarnation and other-universe tales because we have, each of us, seen so many

movies and experienced so much vicariously that it is as though
we have already lived hundreds or even thousands of simultaneous
lives.

The problem with Shirley MacLaine's *Out on a Limb,* especially as dramatized for TV, is not the particular phenomena it
presents; these, after all, are primary spiritual-awakening experiences. It is that the experiences are posed in Hollywood terms,
and ideologized; the account wreaks of "the spiritual advancement
of the rich and famous" — because they are already rich and
famous. No wonder the "stars" of other celestial systems go through
such trouble to contact them. California dumb for sure.

It is "scandalous" that we don't know whether these are
Pleiadian aliens, angels, or evolved forms of ourselves, etc., not
because we have to know in order to act properly but because we
have to know that we cannot know, and that we cannot resolve
them by naming them. The system is finally much more radical
and unpromised than this. (Just because the spiritual master lets
you call him by his first name doesn't mean he isn't dangerous.) [14]

Each of our lives, as written in the skies, has its unique con-
figuration. However, we cannot expect the message to be written
out in the heavens — except insofar as we pass in and out gates
and transits all our lives, subject always to unknown convergences
and divergences, harmonies and discordances; it is our errand,
our life course, to integrate these and deepen them into our souls.
We cannot present ourselves at the altar of the Grand Convergence
and expect to be swept along — instant UFO rescue, or New Age,
or Apocalypse.

Brezsny again:

"O dearest darling God, I confess that I have learned to worship the lies you love the best.

"O God, you eater of cruelty, I confess that I am not *like*
you, I *am* you. . . .

"O God, you pregnant criminal who scorns all my mediocre
desires. . . .

"O God, you wealthy anarchist burning heaven to the
ground. . . .

"O God of so much change I want to puke. . . . "[15]

Without such an exposé and rebellion, the New Age is a tinsel apologism for our cowardice and numbing.

We have no time for someone's glitzy impersonation of a spiritual occasion. When "beings" from outer space warn us in Old Celtic, when women from the Pleiadian Confederacy visit Billy Meier on his farm, when the White Witches of England team with Sri Aurobindo to defeat a house-painter empowered by Satanic aliens, when the atmosphere of the Earth is collapsing and glaciers melting, when the nations of the Earth from Afghanistan to Angola declare peace under the flimsiest of pretexts, when a human face is discovered on the surface of Mars, when extraterrestrials walk through walls to kidnap children, when our astral plane is littered with weird, quarrelling consciousnesses from everywhere else, when the house is haunted and the film fogged, when Men in Black appear at the door, when we have reached the end of all places to quaff oil, bury radioactive waste, dissolve smoke, then we had better stop following Fundamentalist preachers and Hollywood gurus and turn to the oracle within. We live among ghosts and chimeras; yet something alive is addressing us from a locale we have recognized only as Void. It may have been addressing us forever. We do not know what it is. I repeat despite claims of Mayan prophecy and bodies of Martians in the White House, despite trance visits to golden cities and radar trackings of UFOs, predicted earthquakes and second comings—*we do not know what is happening to us; we do not even know who we have been.* It is better to realize that cosmic visitors, flying shamans, and ten-thousand-year-old spirits make no sense all unless we have already crossed the mind-matter barrier but are still asleep.

The cabal of science is dead; soon enough the ugly duckling will take its place. But if we buy the New Age with its superficially glamorous sideshows, we may miss a marvellous phenomenon; in fact, we may miss our own evolution.

1988

THE MIND
OF THE HEART

preface to 1987 edition of *Planet Medicine*

Our crisis of medicine and health care is primarily a crisis of definition. First of all, we have the most basic difficulty understanding and articulating the nature of the disease process, and finding — or even imagining — acceptable cures. Then, we encounter complex systems of medicine and healing operating at different levels of concreteness and contradicting one another's definitions of the same processes and terms — while at the same time each proposing universal holism. We can extricate ourselves only by reexamining our quiescent categories in such a way that their contradictions become energetic, at least on the level of language.

Reexamination *must* be participatory and phenomenological. I do not believe that a sociological or philosophical overview does anything more than repackage traditional categories in the illusion of new paradigms. For instance, a decision to review medicine anthropologically does not eliminate cultural bias or guarantee universal ethics. Likewise, the deconstruction of therapy by conceptual and psycholinguistic models undermines its basis in raw experience; the result is an intellectualized argument rife with its own rigid symptomology (despite the fact that the model may also critique its self-evoked disease). I finally prefer the exercises of Wilhelm Reich to the much more exquisitely reasoned diagnoses of Jacques Lacan et al. if only because the former submerge the body in the somatic criteria of its survival whereas the latter are always subject to the clever manipulations and evasions of the professional persona.

Yet, to by-pass both the medical and academic authorities and to pretend to resolve the crisis by making it spiritual, "holistic" — or both — is a naive overvaluation of our ability to redefine and thereby alter our condition. This overvaluation is the credo of the "holistic health" movement. I am in sympathy with even many of the jazzier alternative systems, but I have trouble with their tendency to present themselves as if coming from authority and as adjudicating all intermediate issues of level and meaning. It is as though, by definition, a vitalistic medicine, like homoeopathy or shamanic chanting, encounters and activates the life force of the organism, which then distributes its "elixir" to every region of body, mind, and spirit. I do not think this is generally true (if true at all). I also do not think its "lie" negates the value of certain so-defined treatments; it does, however, entail simplification of their exaggerated mythologies.

I consider all the present talk (vintage, 1987) about channels, mediums, extraterrestrials, shamanic trances, healing crystals, and chreodes to be relevant and exciting, but I resist being told exactly what any of these things mean, and particularly how they relate on a one-to-one literal basis to our evolution, personal or planetary. Such spiritual authoritarianism is *always* someone else's interpretation of their own experience for their own reasons.

Perhaps these visitations or visions are archetypes of modern chaos perceived in crisis. Perhaps the so-called entities from the Pleiades and elsewhere represent realms of our own being whose manifestations we cannot accept, so project outward into the bigness of outer space. But even if there are real "intruders," I doubt that our situation will be clarified or resolved by science-fiction escapades or harmonic convergences. If aliens cloned our species from their own "protoplasm," as some claim, we have since become so interwoven in the molecular and viral fabric of the Earth we are now inextricable.

In matters of healing, absolutes are inevitably simplistic and counterproductive. People are self-maintaining organisms in continuous interaction with their environment, so, clearly, no illness will ever be one-hundred-per-cent cured, i.e., excised from their living systems. We are charged quanta of tissue, energy, trauma, scars, immunity, aura; every trace of *everything* radiates through the zones of our wholeness, forever.

From the standpoint of modern medicine we are catastrophic diseases in temporary remission, so allopathy is usually a matter of how long to attempt to sustain life; it is almost never a question of meaning. Yet, even as we can never be cured, we are continuously in the process of self-healing. The most fundamental medicine is our own metabolism. Day by day, through our movements, our thoughts, our food — and by night, through the autonomous by-products of our sleep and dreams — we are healing, and that is *always* a question of meaning; i.e., it is a process intrinsic to the individuation of our organism. Even the most heroic medicine merely stimulates and supports that.

For instance, surgery and drugs represent explicit attempts to remove pathologizing agents; their prescribers don't even pretend to affect the heart of the defense mechanism. It is no accident that the largest expanding category of lethal diseases includes those that directly attack our immune response, that dampen or eliminate the power of self-cure in our bodies. AIDS, lupus, arthritis, diabetes, asthma, allergies — even cancer — alert us to turn away from the traditional tools of allopathy, which are mere postponements — treatments often more toxic than their diseases — and toward the vital and immune-oriented systems of homoeopathy, anthroposophy, acupuncture, bioenergetics, and the like.

But whatever we tell ourselves about psyche and spirit, the biophysical aspect of our existence will terminate. We are involved in an esoteric process that transcends ideology and purity of intent. Disease is our metabolic interface with the universe, so indelibly it is the signature of our responsiveness and individuality. It maintains our necessary separateness from the unity of substance at the same time that it is the revolt of nature *against* our exclusivity — an unrelenting attempt to return our body-minds to the anonymous flow. It is our education, unto death.

Anything, after all, is potentially lethal, anything potentially curative, even AIDS and nuclear weapons. As deep as we sink into pathology, that deeply (by definition) are we mobilizing a defense response. Medicine is a cultural and symbolic aspect of that response. But ultimately the treatment transcends its symbols in order to enter unconscious and biological realms.

For us in the twentieth century, technology is the most deadly mirage distracting us from our crisis and its seriousness. It is not only the direct effects (radiation leaks, toxic industrial wastes, antibiotics breeding exotic new germs, etc.) that make us sick, and then keep us from getting well; it is the degree of our mesmerization with the *concept* of technology that prevents us from approaching the problem in an intrinsic way. This is hardly an idiosyncratic failing of medicine. We need look only at the effects of automobiles on habitation and land-use and of nuclear weapons on general political life to see that we invariably prefer a powerful, energy-consuming device to bind the status quo. The collective residue of all our displacements and postponements of responsibility show up in our health — automobiles and nuclear weapons internalized along with everything else — so of course (paradoxically) we want to enact their same machine "magic" on our bodies. This vast, undifferentiated addiction replaces the sanctity and individuation of our own experience.

We declare, "Get rid of this disease!" as though the locus of its interaction with us could be concretized, isolated, and severed. Then (we tell ourselves) we will feel better. Often we simply feel less, thus feel less disease. Often, too, the disease is an externalized aspect of the healing process, and without it we are sicker.

Because disease is always our intrinsic response to an invasion rather than the invasion itself, it delineates our degree of susceptibility and distortion. Because medicine treats personal experience directly and because it embodies the most powerful metaphor for transformation we have, healing becomes a paradigm for both social revolution and self-development, and cannot be simplified or packaged and programmed into shortcuts.

However, when the day-to-day functioning and economic health of society are viewed in terms of static machines, we picture ourselves as unchanging algorithms too — our organs as separately functioning sites in an assembly-line. A check-up becomes a tune-up. It is hard to envision where the epiphenomenon of "mind" is located in such a schema. To the doctor it is probably a troublesome by-product, the alias of systemic activity in the patient; in himself, it is mostly an unexamined version of his professional ego. To the patient the self is usually an innocent observer trapped in a sophisticated vehicle of meat.

The cumulative effect of such latent beliefs in a profit-oriented society is disastrous. Hospitals have come to view patients primarily as investments. A sick individual is not only a mechanism like a clock; he or she is a commodity, a product on an assembly-line. If too much "care" and time are put into the product, the hospital's profit-margin is reduced. The fewer resources that are put into a product, the better the bottom line. So, the goal of treating patients humanely is not only *one step* removed by the mechanization of biology, it is removed *a second step* by the commodization of the machine. If a sick person's insurance profile does not match the disease prognosis, i.e., does not indicate that there will be money available to pay for the full treatment, doctors are advised not to admit the patient if at all possible. A good doctor, by some present definitions, is one who knows how to churn out as many patients in as short a time as possible, and also how to spot unprofitable patients for rejection. Only those patients whose disease conditions fit the model of expensive high-technology diagnosis and remediation are desirable, and then only if either they or their insurance can afford them.

The cures that take place under such a regime are not only symptomatic and mechanical, they are the *cheapest* symptomatic and mechanical solutions that can be legally perpetrated. (It is a supreme irony that Andy Warhol, who turned the assembly-line image into art, was killed by assembly-line health care.) It is not impossible to get adequate and compassionate treatment in this situation, but such treatment would be entirely incidental to the institutional goals — and a certain indigent percentage of the population would be denied even this skimpy and shoddy mode of care.

Near our home is an oral surgeon who recently performed exquisitely as the malefic physician. I met him several years ago when he was recommended by our dentist as the most convenient person to remove the wisdom teeth of our son Robin. We were uncertain that the operation was necessary, but could get no clear opinion either way from a "holistic" dentist. My wife, Lindy, went for the first consultation and must have communicated that I was the more difficult one, for, through her, the surgeon extended an invitation to me to visit him for a quiet chat. In the waiting room he entertained me with a philosophical discussion about medicine, including a virtual litany of holistic catch-words. "I'm your neighbor," he added. "You can call on me night or day."

I was swayed by his humane persona and agreed to the procedure. Then, for the relatively simple operation, Robin was overdosed with sedatives (while the needle-bearing nurse teased him with comments so spooky he had nightmares for months afterwards: "Where's your big vein hiding, Robin?"). He was returned to us unconscious, and remained half-asleep for days, during which time our "friend" either refused to return our calls or berated me for the "primitive belief-system" I had shown in his office. The sale had been made, so the mask was off. Beneath his relentless suaveness dwelled only the rigid allopathic quack, the type of person who never would have become a physician before the era of automation.

I was not overly shocked when, a few weeks ago, a writer who has cancer of the mouth told me of a recent visit to my "neighbor" to have part of his jaw removed. Despite the fact that he was in great pain, the surgery was postponed until October 31st in order to accommodate the doctor's vacation schedule. My friend arrived for the operation to find the surgical assistant dressed in a Halloween costume, sequins on her face. He was not fully sedated because of the danger he might choke on the bone being removed, and during the operation he heard the doctor say: "This job pays for my trip to Tahiti," and "Be sure to get this guy's money before he leaves."

As my friend described it, the surgeon was breaking off chunks of his jaw with a tool about as sophisticated as a pair of pliers and at the same time talking about him as though he couldn't hear.

"Maybe he didn't think I was too bright," he told me. "I guess that's because of the way I was dressed and the state of my finances. If he were a little smarter he would have known that fools don't dress this way either. I felt like the computer HAL, you know in *2001*. They might just as well turn me off. At one point when they were cracking through the jaw, the assistant tells him, 'Now you're cookin.' I looked at her fingernails and saw little skulls painted on them. I felt as though I were suddenly part of some occult ritual. I was, of course; it's this bizarre ritual called American culture."

Dehumanization, however, is a superficial — and even indulgent — response to the complexity of machines and their origin in the collective psyche; it is one more symptom of our general materialism. Modern technology is ultimately a great riddle, and a dismissal of its modes would be an evasion of many of our most profound and disturbing discoveries about the universe and ourselves. These revelations, ranging from the explosive conditions of galaxy formation to chromosomes determining heredity, may prove, one day, to be no more than skewed and partial truths, but they will never be proved "wrong." Furthermore, there is an enlightened and healing aspect to technology (why else have we promoted progress so devotedly these last few centuries?). Unless our destiny as a species (and a planet) points to an ecological "stone age" following a cataclysm instead of journeys to the stars, we should not reject progressive science in its birth throes. In fact, as noted throughout this book, we are inseparable from its crisis and have long ago passed the failsafe point, when renunciation was possible — so we are far better off including a version of technology in our quest for new medicines and meanings.

Holistic medicine is modern medicine too, and it often partakes of the false authority and materialism of technology. I was reminded of this recently when visited by a German practitioner of a form of energetics. He had a machine that combined the diagnostic aspects of Chinese acupuncture, the circumstantial "proof" of Kirlian photography, and the curative mode of Reich's orgone therapy. It was a very provocative and optimistic machine, and probably a useful one. What was intolerable, though, was its bearer's claim that it healed absolutely everything and that other methods of bodywork, polarity, acupuncture, and herbs were now obsolete. When I tried to offer a more subdued assessment, he told me, kindly and patronizingly, that I was simply not informed and thus ignorant of the implications of the breakthrough.

Such claims leave no room for individuality and doubt; they are orthodoxies equal to allopathy. Human beings are not machines or templates that can be spontaneously vitalized, medicinalized, chi-ed, or shamanized into their own higher beings. They are extremely conservative organisms, and their mere contact with a medium, or their reading a book about reincarnation or chanting, or doing a weekend's shamanic or EST exercises, is not going to transform their lives, or even affect each person in the same way. Very concrete, almost miraculous things are possible, but only in subtle ways and with great attention to details and idiosyncrasies. There is not yet a universal medicine or a catchall metaphor for change.

Despite the literal implication of the word "holistic," the human organism is a fragmented entity and must be treated level by level, persona by persona (some levels and personae will not even appear in a lifetime, and cannot be treated). Surgery and drugs effectively treat one level; gestalt therapy, another; Bach flower remedies, another; chiropractic, another; and so on. But because these levels are actually interpenetrating fields — oscillating flows of biomorphic and psychic "energy" — medicines and meanings introduced into one will be transmitted to all. That is the optimism and legitimate promise of holism. However, a medicine will be directly curative only in the level at which it is introduced. What it translates to other levels may be curative insofar as those levels shift within mind-body awareness and call out for their own treatments. One hopes that a homoeopathic or chiropractic treatment will also clear the mind and lead the individual to seek a psychoanalytic or spiritual treatment to continue the healing process, and vice versa. It is possible, though, that a very effective

treatment, even a vitalistic one, may have pathological consequences if it introduces too much energy into a persona that cannot
contain and integrate it. Perhaps this is why Edward Whitmont,
who is both a homoeopath and a Jungian psychologist, prefers not
to use homoeopathy separate of psychoanalysis: He is concerned
about setting in motion forces that the personality will then either
cathect neurotically or suppress.

In direct answer to the question, can a homoeopathic remedy
remove layers of Reichian armor from the forehead and belly?,
I would say, no. I think that somaticized trauma is structured
deeply and rigidly in the mind/body and can be removed only by
a process of breathing, exercise, and imaging akin to the pathways
by which it was incorporated. However, a homoeopathic remedy
could alleviate a digestive ailment associated with belly armor and
thereby participate in the bioenergetic process of its removal. A
potency might also release the miasmatic and dermatological aspect
of a "mask" and so energize the dissolution of facial armor.

Cases of such mutually interactive healing, even including
coarse allopathic treatments, are probably more prevalent than
people realize, because our most fundamental holistic responses
are profoundly unconscious, creating their own presemantic symbols and constructs. All treatments are equalized, their effects
optimized homeostatically. Somewhere within, surgery, flower
potency, breath, and dream meet, and converge. Despite the
medium, all healing is finally spiritual in consequence. That's *how*
it works and *why* it works. Many so-called holistic and spiritual
treatments merely enact a metaphor of this fact in their attempts
to maintain ideological exclusivity. Sometimes everything else
about a treatment fails, except an inner transformation.

The so-called mind-body split that we work holistically to
unify is probably better described as a split between the mind of
the body and the mind of the mind. It is not mind-body as such
because we are *always* separated from the vast unconscious archetypal body. The problem is that we are often pathologically separated from the mind of the body as well. Meditation, various forms
of bodywork (like that of Feldenkrais, Alexander, Lomi School,
etc.), some forms of psychoanalysis, and, even occasionally, more

"physical" therapies like chiropractic and herbs address the mind as body (or the body as mind), that is, open a channel through our moment-to-moment proprioception into the patterns of energy and substance in our organs. If the process is successful, physical and mental change are simultaneous.

This dynamic might be made clearer by our distinguishing between the intellectual mind, which objectifies itself from the phenomena it experiences (in one of its most sophisticated forms, it is the scientific mind), and the mind of the body, which uses its subjective experiences to develop an internal language of feelings and functional connections. When we speak abstractly of the heart and love for instance, we are not attributing characteristics to the physical aorta; we are identifying the charge we feel from the pumping of blood and the deep oxygenation of the organs *and* our capacity to contain and integrate that charge, to translate it into feelings about another person and acts of emotional exchange. The aikido master identifies the same "love" with the harmony of spirals between *uke* and *nage*. When one puts his or her heart into an act, the projection is far more complex than either the semantic metaphor or the life-giving actions of the circulatory system.

Certainly a major failing of Western culture, and industrial civilization in general, is that it cuts off everyone — capitalists as well as workers — from the mind of the heart, i.e., cuts them off not only from the healing but the acts of compassion that arise from there.

1987

LUMINOUS DREAMS

An alchemical dream cycle

Whenever my sense of my own nature is changing I have a series of cosmic dreams, usually over several nights. These involve distant planets, shifts of stars, articulate animals, and profound intimations of life-span and mortality. There is also an alchemical element which invariably grounds the numinous phenomena in mysteriously animated chunks of matter.

In the oldest dream I remember (from about age seven) I am playing with the sorceror's bottles at a long laboratory table. I knock one of them over, and as it begins to break I hurriedly remove it from the table and rush to the bathroom to pour its leaking contents into the toilet bowl. While I am running I spill the fluid and it burns my legs. I am afraid it is poisonous and I am going to die.

At the time, a psychiatrist interpreted this as a dream of wetting my pants. I accepted the interpretation for thirty years until Charles Poncé pointed out an additional (not alternative) meaning of the image: the spilled chemical might be the burning mercurial waters the alchemists experienced on a concrete level. These waters belong to the sorceror; coming from the underworld, they are imprinted with life and death. For a time I handled and experienced them, but most of their fire spilled back or remained in the unconscious. In 1952 the dream led to a child's initiation:

when it was interpreted I learned that my daily self was simply representational and a deeper being within also spoke through me. Even though the doctor's analysis of the burning waters was limited to their role as urine in "wetting," the revelation of their "secret" by a "magus" was mercurial, for it taught me very early that the world itself was made up of radiant symbols buried beneath my simple life. The problem of "keeping dry" is also an alchemical matter insofar as "toilet training" requires bringing consciousness to the autonomic realms of the body.

The childhood dream was brought back to mind by a different version of it that occurred in 1981:

I am returning to the dark brownstone in Greenwich Village where the old doctor practiced. (He had been dead twenty-four years.) I have to pee very badly, and I stumble into a bathroom so dark I cannot see the toilet. As the urine hits the "water," I smell sulphur and then I hear hydrochloric acid bubbling in the bowl. I rationalize that it is not my pee but a substance in the toilet, and in any case the gurgling stops. Then, as I am leaving the room I hear the sound again, like sizzling rice soup, and I realize my upper lip is burning from having been splattered. I am wondering why there is a burning element in my urine, and I think that I must tell this dream to Poncé.

The result was a startling reinterpretation of the childhood dream. But no doubt these fire of waters come to the surface periodically for reasons of revelation.

A prior alchemical dream followed my taking of homoeopathic phosphorus for a digestive ailment in Vermont in 1976. In a fever that night I dreamed (or half-awake saw) my body stretched out before me on the bed as on a doctor's examination table. Thin tubes flowed down from my left and right eyes, meandering in my torso and crossing each other in the area of my diaphragm, ultimately connecting to my testicles opposite the eyes from which they began. In the left eye's tube flowed silver liquid, and the symbol for the moon hung like an aura below my right testicle, and in the right eye's tube a golden liquid was running (although at times it seemed red), and the symbol for the sun shone below my

left testicle. These were perhaps partial representations of the *Ida*
and *Pingala*, the psychic nerves running down the left and right
sides of the Kundalini subtle body. At the time of the "vision" I
felt strong but dizzy, and I understood that I would be sick for
a long time while the medicine was working. In fact I was sick
for almost two months in the time approaching my thirty-first
birthday, but the illness directly led to my meeting Edward Whitmont, a doctor immersed in the alchemical tradition.

Four years later I had a similar ailment, and on its final night,
after a day in heavy surf on the beach in San Diego, I dreamed
that I was carrying my own dead body out of a prison and solemnly
burying it in the ebb tide under the Moon. The horror that it was
my body was countered by my amazement that I was still alive
to do this. Two months later this dream led me, through Whitmont, to a year of work in the alchemical mysteries with Charles
Poncé. The ultimate healing was mediated through a dream cycle
in January of 1981:

There is a mound, maybe a dead body. I am supposed to fertilize
it. Coming down from the sky in a column and passing directly
through me are the letters of the Hebrew alphabet, one by one
and moving very fast like insects. They are tiny and imprinted
in black. The shaft seems to form diagonally out in front of me
in the distance, but it enters the top of my head. I sense that these
are seeds, and I am going to fertilize the mound with them. I will
split it open with the force from my penis. I feel an electrical buzz
pass into me suddenly with the letters, and I cannot move. I see
the letter *lamed*. I wake up.

Falling back asleep I am standing in an unknown place something like the colored fountain in Flint, Michigan. Huge chunks
of wood are piled up in the basin of the fountain, a disorganized
heap whose clutter extends like a tower with the lower boards supporting a platform in the heavens. The wood is very very old. It
has been undisturbed since before man came to the New World,
and even long before that. It has almost no weight left in it, no
gravity. A row of peoples has formed in front of the fountain, and
one by one men and women are stepping into the lumber and
bathing. I am in line and being pushed forward. I try to escape

because it looks dark and cold, but I cannot get out of the line, and I find myself in the water, which is very thick. The boards are light as air. I am struggling to hang onto them and pull myself up, but they are too insubstantial to climb. I turn and shout for the others to retreat because the pool is collapsing. But the person ahead of me says that I should ascend, that I cannot sink. "Don't you realize that this water has been undisturbed for hundreds of thousands of years," says a voice. "It has nothing left. You cannot possibly drown." Since there is no way out, I start pulling myself up rapidly like a lemur through gravityless space, springing from plank to plank. At the same time I seem to be going down into the water, or pulling myself up into new water. It is heavy substance, and I don't want to be contaminated by it. I sink down through the quality of the wood and the water, but I do not drown. I seem to emerge on the top plaza.

It is no wonder I am afraid. First I am asked to fertilize the absolutely mute mound which has not yet been touched by consciousness, and I am given the magic stream of original language with which to do it. Then I am asked to bathe in the raw waters and materia of which I am myself made. Six nights later the mound reappears in an altered condition.

I am on an airplane flight across the country, but it is also like a bus and the passengers are able to talk to the pilot. It only becomes clear we are in the air when we pass over the scene of an old accident — far off to the right behind a wooded hill and close to the ocean. It is less like a crash, on closer inspection, than like an earth mound heaped up and shaped like a plane with part of its right wing missing. Later in the dream the pilot recalls the ancient crash of which this mound of dirt is a fossil. No one was killed, but there are people walking around with no brains or minds from the force, and it is considered a great tragedy. Although the pilot can remember it, the accident happened so long ago that the site has turned to stone.

The next night I am in a deep and dark forest with Benjamin Lo, the t'ai chi master. We are headed toward the lake, and I am tossing aside large branches of trees that have fallen. I am wishing I had a chainsaw to cut them into firewood. But Ben is involved in what seems to be a piece of wood and turns out to be a living wormlike entity — a fish, a frozen fish still alive. It is gradated pink and white with cartilage in the center. It has an obvious fish exterior with scales. I ask him what it is, and he holds it toward me, saying, "This weighs more than a pallet of books." He cuts it into three pieces across its length, as though such a division were natural. I want to feel how heavy it is, but I am not empty enough. It is of neutron star density, and he is able to hold it because of his mastery of *chi*. I look at it in his hands. It is solid, rich, and complex; it is alive and dead both, wood and worm. It is shaped like the mound. I sense the darkness all around us. It has just rained, and soft pink salamanders have come out; like glow-worms, they are the only light. This is a hopeful moment; a dream ally, one not fluent in English, has come to share the burden with me, to divide it and reveal some of its nature.

(A month later I dream of being in the same forest, alone. It is even blacker than before, and I sense that I am standing in the night of the creation, the night behind the night — above me certainly but also beneath me as my feet sink into unknown dense substance with every step. I sense omniscience everywhere. I try to find the cottage from which I wandered. I suddenly see new moons appearing around a planet; there is a meteor shower rushing toward me through the stars, and They are Searching for Me. I hide in the grass, but slowly a few of Them break ranks and come toward me; UFOs, giant faces leap out at me until I cannot look at them anymore and awake.)

One night after being with Ben Lo in the secret forest I dream of being back at our house from years ago in Maine. We have returned to repair something. Yet it is indistinguishable from our present house in California. The work must be done under the structure in a very cramped space. It has something to do with making the soil more fertile. Vegetables have grown in the winter, but they look more like gems than living things. It is snowing, and the plants stand out brightly in the ice. The forest seems to be growing under the house. The space is cluttered also with cartons of books. I am working with a hoe when I uncover a huge chunk of apple, a slab about 2½ feet long, a foot and a half across, and six inches thick. It is pure juicy apple shaped in a prism. I think this should be broken up, and remember that there are instructions. I begin hacking at it with the hoe, but this has no effect. I am about to abandon it when I get the idea of cutting a groove into its surface. I work with a sharp tool, and the apple crumbles fairly easily, leaving a slot. Then I strike it with the hoe in order to split its surface; instead it splits beneath the surface so that I have two long thinner slabs of apple which I place in the soil under the house. I think it is a waste to fertilize ground in shadow, but apparently the apple was meant for such a purpose. Now I look out from under the house and see that it is a garage or barn, and the real house is across the field. A tiny white rabbit has gotten loose where I am working, and it is running toward the house carrying children's underpants in its mouth.

The dense object has become softer and tastier, and it has given rise to a garden of jewels. It splits only along *its own* nature, not by the nature I would assign it. A living thing arises and carries out a prank; something mercurial and joyful. The following night the dense object has become a medicine:

I go to bed with a bellyache and dream of having homoeopathic Nux prescribed for me. It has formed not in the usual little white balls but as cubed chunks with smaller cubes coming out of the faces of mother cubes in all the directions. There is a hidden spiral motif so that it resembles the crystals of galena lead but is still white and crumbly. I put the medicine in my mouth, and it tastes thick and insoluble. I am not sure I ever swallow it, but my symptoms diminish instantly. I am now translating the density inward as sensation.

That same night I dream of visiting a woman with whom I used to do work on breathing. During our dream session she gives birth. I must help the infant out, and in the process I become merged with the birth waters, become the baby, and kiss her on her lips which are crusted with salt crystals. The baby squirts out and slides around on the bed until both of us, using our arms, corral the slippery thing. Then she picks it up and talks to it in a hoarse babble. Something has finally been born — not a symbol, but actual material out of the unconscious depths.

Two nights later I am at a vacation place in Florida. I am standing on the beach when a gigantic flat boat comes by. It is not a boat so much as a huge piece of rough unfinished wood with masses of people standing on it. I am with my family, and we are told that we can ride on it and be taken around the peninsula out into the southern sea. We stand on this flat form, rushing through the waves as through the sky. The shore moves in the distance. This is the first time anyone has seen these jungle lands; they are a new unexplored continent. The water comes in great rushes and waves upon the beach and fills it with tiny animals. Everything now is swarming with life.

Stellar Objects

Returning to the village in Vermont where I once lived, I am wandering toward the river at night. I learn from an undisclosed source that I am now in the Solar System. Immediately I begin to look about for planets. I do not know what region I am in. Suddenly I see a huge bright object spinning in the front yard of a house by the river. I recognize it instantly from its markings as the moon Ganymede of Jupiter. It is radiant, enormous, and intricately engraved, and, as it spins, I see all the features of the Voyager photographs. Yet, it is somehow contained in this front yard. Now that I know where I am, I begin to look for Jupiter itself. I suspect it must be over the large hill that rises out of town to the mountains. In fact, I am drawn in that direction by an immense gravity. I try to look through the trees, but the forest is as dense as lead, and I can only feel the presence of Jupiter beyond.

I start at once to climb in darkness, and I am very careful. I feel that at any misstep I can stumble and fall into Jupiter. The climb is perilous, as if I am walking along a mountain ledge overlooking the sea. I wonder if there are any other moons about, and I turn to see a tiny ball spinning rapidly in a bush in front of a house. I think, "How cute. That's the tiny fifteenth moon." It is minute compared to Ganymede, but just as fiery and radiant. I realize that dozens of these moons might be scattered in the bushes all around here, and I feel as though I am a child in an Easter

Egg Hunt.

The heaviness pulls me up the hill, and, suddenly, through the trees, I see an enormous limb of brilliance. It is so overwhelming that it seems literally to blow me back. But I push on, as if I am floating in space. I see the broad bands of the planet, and I struggle to get out of its way.

A voice is suddenly telling me that I don't understand gravitation at all. "These are not the real planets," it says. "They are painted balls." I understand that it is speaking about the actual planets in space; it is saying that they themselves are only painted balls and that these replicas of them are mere symbols of the internal planets. There is another gravity, inside gravity, which is the real core of substance. I feel a wholeness and a bigness, as if all that cannot be connected or realized in a lifetime is joined in a unity of self for this one moment.

March 19–20, 1981. I am with Spock and Kirk in a small spacecraft, having to escape from our exploding mothership; we are also using its energy to propel us to the other end of the Solar System. The damaged ship turns out to be wedged in between my father's old house and a grove of trees. I run into the house and see a control panel. The sky on the screen is a model of the Solar System with all the planets and moons. Then it changes. Suddenly I am at the edge of the Solar disk looking down. I notice innumerable planets and moons, though I can't even locate the known ones. I am supposed to find Pluto for us, but I see all sorts of other configurations, including stars among clouds. Something tells me that I am looking at new unknown patterns, objects that have no names yet. I locate the tiny whirling outer planet, but it is called Oedipus not Pluto even though no one has seen it yet — meaning not that astronomers have prepared a name in expectation of its discovery but that there is a planetary form out beyond our senses already named Oedipus. I realize it is a revenge on Freud and his symbols, labelling this new planet with his most obvious primal symbol to indicate that it is totally nonsymbolic; if it is actually Oedipus, and if its dream identity is a subterfuge, then there is nothing left it could stand for. It is very small and whizzing along, throwing off particles of sparkling dust in its orbit; I can see the whole com-

plication of the inner Solar System back through it. It is an absolute product of the Sun's gravity. It is the proof that the dream
is autonomous and that its symbols come to an end in the twentieth century at the limits of the stars.

August 8–9, 1981. My kids and I are on a cliff overlooking the
ocean. Cosmic changes are taking place; stars and moons are moving. I have the fear of sudden atomic warfare bursting out of the
sky, but this anxiety is transcended by the wonder of what is taking place. I am watching actual constellations being born, their
stars realigning into place. A very thin crescent moon is arched
at an unlikely angle. It has a double quality about it. I'm not sure
whether that means it suggests an inner dimension or there are
two moons moving around each another in thin crescent shapes
like wire tops spinning. Now a guide is there explaining it all to
a group that stands with him, watching. The scene is the coast
of Maine (proven by a stock lighthouse). The man says the moon
is in the right position (or at least the secondary right position —
perhaps not quartered enough) for the fish to come. So, the fish
come, and they are like lightning. There are two of them, and
just as I described the moons almost revolving around each other,
the fish do. They are not fish. They are whales, but they are not
whales either. They leap out of the water setting up complex fields
about each other; they disappear and reappear. Only their spouts
make them whales. They are actually jagged bolts of radiation,
or luminous thin strips of light, tangled more like tree branches
than photons. They appear maybe three or four times crossing our
field of view. Each time they "leap" out of the water, radiate about
each other, and disappear. The man is discussing their behavior
and what lucky timing it is that we see them at just this moon.
I realize how steep the cliff is, how deep the water, and suddenly
I am afraid. I call Miranda (my daughter) back from the edge
to sit by me.

August 21–2, 1981. Robin (my son) and I are wandering through
the basement of my old junior high school building where he finds
two old paintings that are very valuable. One of them is a Giotto,
the other a Klee. At first I think he has just found some neat things,

including a radio he has stuck up on a pole by the entrance to our garage at home as a beacon to pick up news of war. The Giotto painting has Christ on a cross, and the cross is so incredibly golden it virtually gleams. The Klee stands out less well, but is made up of lines forming different colored squares fading into and out of each other within a larger geometrical design. It appears that neither of these works of art were known before Robin found them, but now people are clamoring to see them and to force us to decide how to protect them. Days pass in the dream, and night after night we are in a dangerous situation where thieves are trying to break into our house and take the paintings. Slowly, the sense of their value sinks in, but, at the same time, their actual physical appearance begins to deteriorate and they become less spectacular, more common. I am beginning to worry they are fake, and I think we should fly to New York, take them to a museum, and find out what they are worth. I am on a subway when a woman wants to see what I am carrying. She pulls away the plastic protection in a very grabby way, reaches in, and tries to break off part of the Giotto, which has now turned into a Navajo-like hanging of strings and other artifacts on a frame. She succeeds in tearing loose one of the strings. I shout at her: "Don't you know what this is worth!" And I point to the center where I now see there is a clustering of solid gold objects like coins or discs from which the strings hang down; this area is so newly formed that wet alchemical debris still clings to the discs like yolk. She is miffed and indicates that she is entitled to a souvenir.

November 3–4, 1982. I am visiting an old folks' home, but it is more like a huge institution of learning, a college. Many of my uncles from childhood are there, but they have become blind or partially blind. It is daytime, but the night sky is visible through the blue. I see strange streaks of stars like cirrus clouds. Then one of the old uncles — a lawyer from Brooklyn — takes out a book he can apparently read without seeing. He says we must trace our present position in it. He turns the pages and allows me to view the stars as they are actually configured in three dimensions. There is a huge Mongol warrior's head, and successive photographs show that, as we transit it and look down upon it (year after year and century by century), more of the exquisite detail of the face, made up of trillions of stars, is revealed. The astrogeography is so complex and interwoven it would take thousands of lifetimes to examine it all, but our exploration is condensed into the dream. We turn the pages and view its holographic entirety. I think it is crucially significant that the stars have sculpted such a perfect figure in space. Then my uncle turns the pages of the book back to our present zone with its cirrus streaks and asks for my interpretation. It seems obvious that the Earth not only looks directly upon but is entering a disturbed zone. I tell them that we will leave behind only monuments to ourselves (like tombstones and bones). And then I realize our thoughts remain too, even after cremation — that this complex sector of space requires we remain in the Mongol warrior's head, still conscious, until our destiny is resolved.

THE HOMELESS

What is remarkable about our time is not how much but how little we know.

We think we do not understand UFOs, or acupuncture needles, or poltergeists, or quasars, but these are child's games compared to the true Sphinx.

We struggle to resolve national debt, ozone layer, greenhouse sky, trade deficit, gridlock, but bankruptcy is primal and contentless. Our machines operate on borrowed time, and to what mysterious stranger will we someday owe everything?

Science seeks the source of matter in equations generated by stars and the remains of stars. Observations are turned into integers and signs whose own origin is as obscure as that of the stars, and different. We have no sense of the context of these numbers, how they bind us, what abstract formality they promote. In our knee-jerk advocacy of a quantitative universe we are not even aware of a problem. $E = MC^2$, for sure, but in relation to what?; formed out of symbols and languages, how?

The proposal within physics to explain the universe is delusionary; the assorted mobs and cartels could care less, for they rule the universe of meaning, of the shaman and the wild pig.

We do not understand the extinction of the dinosaurs, the Bermuda Triangle, the origin of AIDS, the assassination of John Kennedy (or its weird parallels to the assassination of Abraham Lincoln), or the fireball that blasted Siberia in 1908. We think we know why the space shuttle exploded and who shot down the KAL jet. At a meeting of the American Anthropological Association it was declared, irrefutably, that Carlos Castaneda had invented the shaman Don Juan.

We do not know Pol Pot, Khomeini, Gorbachev. We do not even know Ronald Reagan, though we poured the collective presidency into his being.

We do not understand the rain-forest or the ozone layer, the whales or sea gulls.

We do not comprehend the Shroud of Turin, but then we do not suspect how many different humanoid apes preceded us, and each other, or how deeply they led us into this forest of numbers.

We do not fathom how Nazis could have prevailed in an advanced nation in a civilized century. Yet slaughterhouses of sentient beings are everywhere. The Earth has become a mechanized flesh and blood factory.

Cocaine? Crack? Child pornography?

Yin/Yang? Shadow. Light. Who are we kidding?

For every act of science unveiling the universe, a compensatory intuition drives us deeper into mystery.

As sexuality becomes explicit, something else becomes obscure. This is axiomatic. Fucking and masturbation occur on stage, bondage and orgies in suburbia. Businessmen and -women do not even drop their personae as they pleasure themselves and each other ritually. Desire is now business; business, desire. Pedophiles act freely — ordinary fathers, coaches, school-teachers, without an awareness of betrayal, because permission is simply procedural. Back in the 50's in mainstream America, extramarital sex was still an exotic taboo; now middle-class people advertise their erotic tastes for each other in newspapers. The compulsive religion of the moral majority, the strategies of corporate merger represent the same "looking out for number one" grab at ego-rapture.

But the mystery, the impalpable allure that was once a sexual episode is now the stuff of life itself. When the fantasy of desire is charmed to the surface, the mystery of eros sinks to the heart. Potentially limitless trysts once formed an unspoken backdrop to marriages; in fact, to lives. Now some of those people are looking for lovers at bars, meeting young underclass prostitutes on the street, but the fantasy is not resolved, merely transposed.

It is our hearts that are closed as we go about our businesses. Something beyond desire now haunts the world. Why else would we return to Nazi Germany for redemption?; why continue to clone the Bomb?; why run no one against no one in elections? Why make a pretense of progress and enlightenment in this miasma?

The homeless are no surprise. They are not withdrawn from reality; they have simply retreated to where no more harm can be done, no more tricks can be played. By their presence they establish ideology. They are our scientists, but their specialty is not substance. What passes them on the street is a clutter of hungers, petty jobs, fake resolutions. By making themselves powerless and brief, they cast the spell of cornucopia back over the masses.

Theirs is not a sophisticated desire or sly strategy of sensuality; it is a pure hunger, the sense that the cauldron is empty. They would rather sit and let the rain of futility gradually work in to their bones.

Some become angry, hard, and throw themselves at the walkers; they are waiting for Godot too, less patiently. Others are as soft as feather, and there is no excuse not to give them some of the coins we find ourselves carrying—the make-believe integers that turn to gold in their hands.

Because they are too many (and I am distracted), I run on by them quickly, refusing to notice. An image registers: one toothless black man, his hand silently out in the crowd, his hat falling off, his sad face irrefutable. I stop and go back. Handing him the coins I feel suddenly that the borders of the city are visible, the cold is real, the light on the street an actual light.

I know the ego doesn't survive. If it did, this would be a demonish eternity, for us as for the street people. I know the ego doesn't survive, though at times I think I want that more than anything. I fear death openly. But I see in the beggar's face that consciousness is no meager thing. We share a pinched, luminous reality as ghosts.

Consciousness will not be obliterated, for consciousness *is* the universe. The part of me I know the least, will go on. These images of a winter's night will not be kept in the holograph's heart — the rain on the beggars along storefront walls, the feeling of unexplored depths, the now-acrid, now-sweet obscurity in me, that even my attempt to locate and feel radiates as petals of deeper, more devious obscurities — a memory of childhood, a fragment of a tunc I can't place, the cold that wants warm, the tug toward home, all together, all making me up this one moment — that will be dashed on rocks harsher than either atoms or stars, because atoms and stars are abstractions that transform nothing.

My hope is their hope — that this will all be made into a robe of the finest light. (Don't be fooled into assuming they have given up hope or that the rest of us have been spared their fate).

I don't need angels or stories through eternity, and I don't expect the timeless void of transcendence or a merger with a superconsciousness. I want the obscurity that nothing will touch in the rain.

1988

Notes

Sea Wall

"Sea Wall" was written as a preface to an autobiographical narrative *New Moon*. It is no longer part of the unpublished manuscript.

The New Age

1. Samuel Beckett, *Molloy*. New York: Grove Press, 1955.

Waiting for the Martian Express

The style of invention in this essay is to put real quotes, or at least quotes from real sources, between quotation marks, and fictional quotes between dashes, sometimes combining the two within the same body of text.

1. Andrija Puharich, *Beyond Telepathy*. Garden City, New York: Anchor Press/Doubleday and Company, 1973, pp. 33–4.

2. Andrija Puharich, *Uri: A Journal of the Mystery of Uri Geller*. Garden City, New York: Anchor Press/Doubleday and Company, 1974, pp. xxvi–xxvii.

3. Philip Wheelwright (editor), *The Presocratics*. Indianapolis: The Odyssey Press, 1966, pp. 162 and 160 (fragments 13 and 7).

4. Ibid., p. 73 (fragment 57).

5. Puharich, *Uri*, p. 152.

6. Ibid., p. 153.

7. Ibid., pp. 153–4.

8. J. R. R. Tolkien, *The Lord of the Rings*. New York: Ballantine Books, © J. R. R. Tolkien, 1965.

9. Puharich, *Uri*, pp. 152–3.

10. Ibid., p. 189.

11. Wheelwright (editor), op. cit., p. 70 (fragment 93).

12. Puharich, *Uri*, p. 154.

13. Edgar Rice Burroughs, *A Princess of Mars*. New York: Ballantine Books, 1963 (originally published in 1912), p. 60.

Third World Wipeout

The style of invention in this essay is to put real quotes, or at least quotes from real sources, between quotation marks, and fictional quotes between dashes, sometimes combining the two within the same body of text. The dates and page numbers for the sources were not retained.

1. Eldridge Cleaver, *Rolling Stone* interview.

2. ibid.

3. ibid.

4. Israel Regardie, *The Eye in the Triangle: An Interpretation of Aleister Crowley*. Saint Paul, Minnesota: Llewellyn Publications, 1970.

The Brazilian Master in Berkeley

1. John F. Gilbey, *The Way of a Warrior*. Berkeley, California: North Atlantic Books, 1982, pp. 47–56.

Some material in this essay appeared in Bira Almeida (Mestre Acordeon), *Capoeira: A Brazilian Art Form* (Berkeley, California: North Atlantic Books, 1986) and in Richard Grossinger and Lindy Hough (editors), *Nuclear Strategy and the Code of the Warrior: The Faces of Mars and Shiva in the Crisis of Human Survival* (North Atlantic Books, 1984).

About the Bomb

This essay was most of the preface to Richard Grossinger and Lindy Hough (editors), *Nuclear Strategy and the Code of the Warrior: The Faces of Mars and Shiva in the Crisis of Human Survival* (North Atlantic Books, 1984).

1. Rob Brezsny, *Images are Dangerous*. Santa Cruz, California: Jazz Press, 1983, p. 13. Reprinted in Richard Grossinger (editor), *Planetary Mysteries* (Berkeley, California: North Atlantic Books, 1986, pp. 154–5).

2. Thomas Powers, *Thinking About the Next War*. New York: New American Library, 1982, pp. 136–7.

3. John Le Carré, *The Spy Who Came in from the Cold*. New York: Avenel Books, 1983.

4. Rob Brezsny, op. cit., p. 13 in *Images are Dangerous* and p. 155 in *Planetary Mysteries*.

Aboriginal Elder Speaks in Ojai

1. Géza Róheim, *The Riddle of the Sphinx*, translated from the German by R. Money-Kyrle. New York: Harper and Row: 1974, pp. 58–9.

2. W. E. H. Stanner, "The Dreaming." Indianapolis: Bobbs-Merrill Reprint Series in the Social Sciences, A-214; reprinted from *Australian Signpost*, Melbourne, 1956, p. 52.

Easy Death

The quotes are all from Da Free John, *Easy Death: Talks and Essays on the Inherent and Ultimate Transcendence of Death and Everything Else* (Clearlake, California: The Dawn Horse Press, 1983).

The Face on Mars

This foreword appeared in Richard C. Hoagland, *The Monuments of Mars: A City on the Edge of Forever* (Berkeley, California: North Atlantic Books, 1987).

1. Richard Grossinger (editor), *Planetary Mysteries* (North Atlantic Books, 1986, pp. 46–7). This is taken from the postscript to an interview with Richard C. Hoagland (pp. 7–47).

Giving Them a Name

This lecture was given at the "Angels, Aliens, and Archetypes" Conference, sponsored by Omega Foundation, Palace of Fine Arts, San Francisco, November, 1987.

1. Jule Eisenbud, Interview by Richard Grossinger (January 8, 1972), in Richard Grossinger (editor), *Ecology and Consciousness* (Berkeley, California: North Atlantic Books, 1978, pp. 168–9).

A Critical Look at the New Age

1. Arthur M. Young, *The Reflexive Universe: Evolution of Consciousness*. Mill Valley, California: Robert Briggs Associates, 1984.

2. Ibid., p. 11.

3. Da Free John, *The Transmission of Doubt: Talks and Essays on the Transcendence of Scientific Materialism through Radical Understanding*. Clearlake, California: The Dawn Horse Press, 1984, pp. 265–7.

4. Claude Lévi-Strauss, *The Savage Mind*, translated from the French. Chicago: The University of Chicago Press, 1966, p. 95.

5. Colin Wilson, *Afterlife: An Investigation of the Evidence for Life After Death*. New York: Doubleday and Company, 1987, p. 110.

6. Ibid., pp. 136–7.

7. These come from a variety of sources, including: Mel Noel, "UFO Lecture" (1966) in Richard Grossinger (editor), *Io*, No. 4 *(Alchemy Issue)*, Ann Arbor, Michigan, 1967, p. 114; Lt. Col. Wendelle C. Stevens (editor), *UFO . . . Contact from the Pleiades,* Volume 1 (Phoenix, Arizona: Genesis III Productions, 1979), no page number; and Jacques Vallee, *The Invisible College* (New York: E. P. Dutton, 1975, p. 83).

8. Jacques Vallee, *The Invisible College*, pp. 143 and 145.

9. Ibid., p. 153.

10. Jule Eisenbud, *Parapsychology and the Unconscious*. Berkeley, California: North Atlantic Books, 1983, pp. 241–2.

11. Rob Brezsny, "I Love America," from the *World Entertainment War* tape cassette by Rob Brezsny, Santa Cruz, California: World Entertainment War, 1987.

12. Doris Lessing, *The Wind Blows Away Our Words: A Firsthand Account of the Afghan Resistance*. New York: Vintage Books/Random House, 1987, pp. 16–17.

13. Robert A. Monroe, *Far Journeys*. Garden City, New York: Dolphin Books/Doubleday and Company, 1985.

14. Source unknown, but passed on by Ruth Terrill, the cover artist for this book.

15. Rob Brezsny, op. cit.

The Mind of the Heart

This essay appeared within the 1987 author's preface to *Planet Medicine: From Stone Age Shamanism to Post-Industrial Healing*, (Berkeley, California: North Atlantic Books, 1987).

Luminous Dreams

These dreams were collected in the essay "The Dream Work" by Richard Grossinger, which appeared in Richard Russo (editor), *Dreams are Wiser Than Men* (Berkeley, California: North Atlantic Books, 1987, pp. 191–246).

Bibliography

Almeida, Bira. *Capoeira: A Brazilian Art Form*. Berkeley, California: North Atlantic Books, 1986.

Beckett, Samuel. *Molloy*. New York: Grove Press, 1955.

Brezsny, Rob. *Images are Dangerous*. Santa Cruz: Jazz Press, 1983.

_____. "I Love America," from *World Entertainment War*. Santa Cruz: World Entertainment War, 1987.

Burroughs, Edgar Rice. *A Princess of Mars*. New York: Ballantine Books, 1963.

Da Free John. *Easy Death*. Clearlake, California: The Dawn Horse Press, 1983.

_____. *The Transmission of Doubt*. Clearlake, California: The Dawn Horse Press, 1984.

Eisenbud, Jule. "Interview" with Richard Grossinger (January 8, 1972), in *Ecology and Consciousness*, North Atlantic Books, 1978.

_____. *Parapsychology and the Unconscious*. Berkeley, California: North Atlantic Books, 1983.

Gilbey, John. *The Way of the Warrior*. Berkeley, California: North Atlantic Books, 1982.

Grossinger, Richard. *Embryogenesis: From Cosmos to Creature*. Berkeley, California: North Atlantic Books, 1986.

_____. *Martian Homecoming at the All-American Revival Church*. Plainfield, Vermont: North Atlantic Books, 1974.

_____. *The Night Sky* (revised edition). Los Angeles. Jeremy P. Tarcher, 1988.

_____. *Planet Medicine: From Stone Age Shamanism to Post-Industrial Healing* (revised edition). Berkeley, California: North Atlantic Books, 1987.

_____. *The Slag of Creation*. Plainfield, Vermont: North Atlantic Books, 1975.

_____. *The Unfinished Business of Doctor Hermes*. Plainfield, Vermont: North Atlantic Books, 1976.

_____ (editor). *Planetary Mysteries*. Berkeley, California: North Atlantic Books, 1986.

Hoagland, Richard C. *The Monuments of Mars: A City on the Edge of Forever*. Berkeley, California: North Atlantic Books, 1987.

Le Carré, John. *The Spy Who Came in from the Cold*. New York: Avenel Books, 1982.

Lessing, Doris. *The Wind Blows Away Our Words: A Firsthand Account of the Afghan Resistance*. New York: Vintage Books/Random House, 1987.

Lévi-Strauss, Claude. *The Savage Mind,* translated from the French. Chicago: University of Chicago Press, 1966.

Noel, Mel. "UFO Lecture," from Richard Grossinger (editor), *Io,* No. 4 *(Alchemy Issue),* Ann Arbor, Michigan, 1967.

Monroe, Robert. *Far Journeys.* Garden City, New York: Doubleday and Company, 1985.

Powers, Thomas. *Thinking about the Next War.* New York: New American Library, 1982.

Puharich, Andrija. *Beyond Telepathy.* Garden City, New York: Anchor Books/Doubleday and Company, 1973.

_____. *Uri.* Garden City, New York: Anchor Press/Doubleday and Company, 1974.

Regardie, Israel. *The Eye in the Triangle: An Interpretation of Aleister Crowley.* Saint Paul: Llewellyn Publications, 1970.

Róheim, Géza. *The Riddle of the Sphinx,* translated from the German by R. Money-Kyrle. New York: Harper and Row, 1974.

Russo, Richard (editor). *Dreams are Wiser Than Men.* Berkeley, California: North Atlantic Books, 1987.

Stevens, Wendelle. *UFO . . . Contact from the Pleiades,* Volume 1. Phoenix: Genesis III Publications, 1979.

Vallee, Jacques. *The Invisible College.* New York: E. P. Dutton, 1975.

Wilson, Colin. *Afterlife: An Investigation of the Evidence for Life After Death.* New York: Doubleday and Company, 1987.

Young, Arthur M. *The Reflexive Universe.* Mill Valley, California: Robert Briggs Associates, 1984.

Index

Richard Grossinger is a native of New York City and a graduate of Amherst College and the University of Michigan from which he received a doctorate in Anthropology. He has taught at the University of Southern Maine and Goddard College in Vermont and is the co-founder and Publisher of North Atlantic Books in Berkeley, California. Other recent titles by him include: *Planet Medicine, The Night Sky,* and *Embryogenesis.* He has also edited a number of anthologies, including *The Temple of Baseball, The Alchemical Tradition in the Late Twentieth Century, Nuclear Strategy and the Code of the Warrior,* and *Planetary Mysteries.*